AF615652

Sea Music
Anthony Caro

Sea Music

Anthony Caro

Ridinghouse

Jim Aitchison is a composer and artist and an Associate Lecturer at the Academy of Music and Theatre Arts, Falmouth University.

Stephen Feeke is an art historian and is a Director of the New Art Centre, Roche Court Sculpture Park.

Alastair Sooke is art critic and columnist for *The Daily Telegraph* and contributes to a number of other magazines and journals as well as BBC television and radio.

David Ward is an artist working in a wide range of media. He co-curated *Seeing Round Corners* at Turner Contemporary, Margate in 2016.

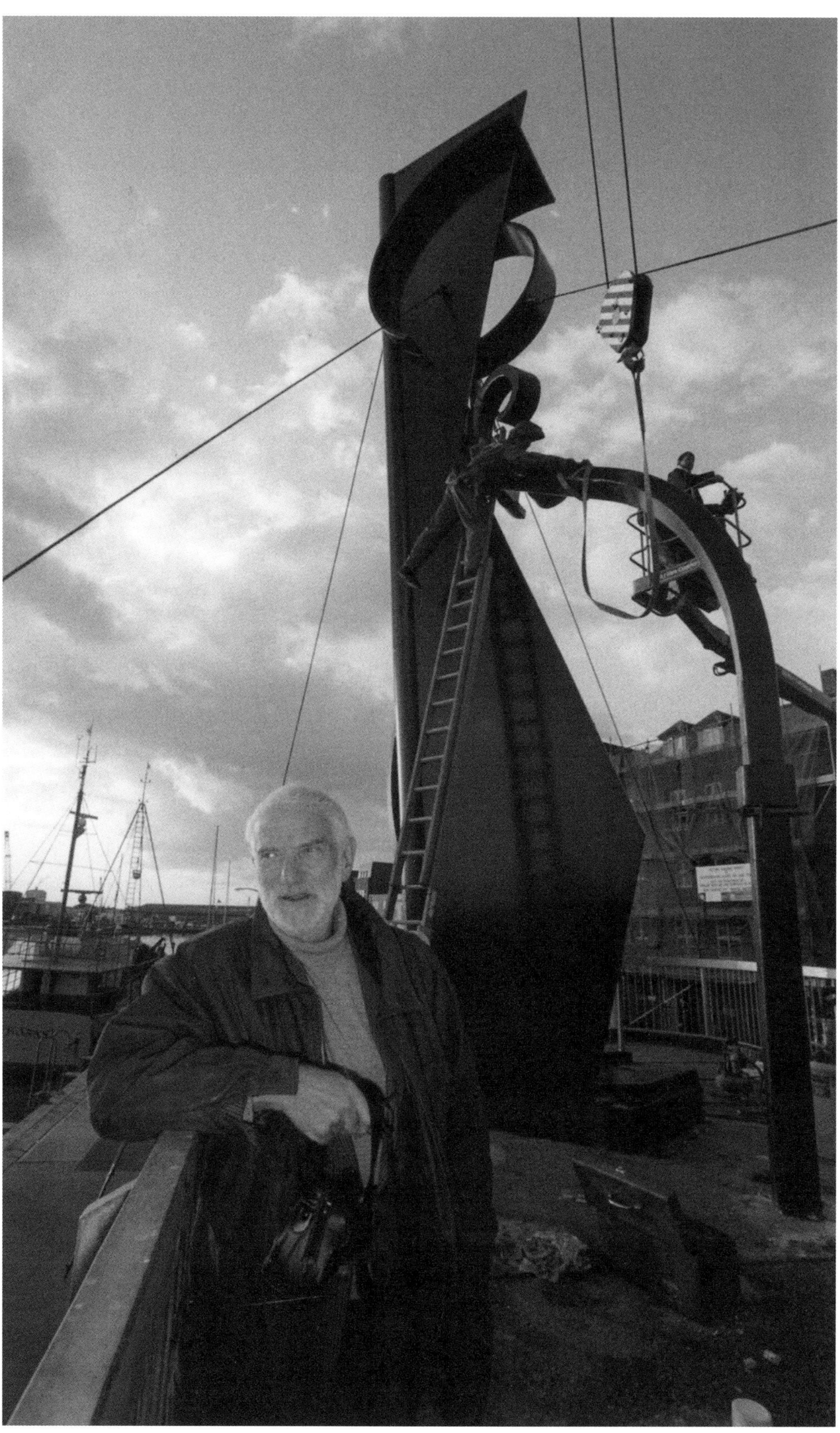

Anthony Caro during the installation of *Sea Music*, October 1991.
Photo: *Bournemouth Daily Echo*

Foreword

Michael Spender

In 1991, when Anthony Caro's *Sea Music* was officially launched by Lord Palumbo, completion of Antony Gormley's *Angel of the North* was seven years away. *Sea Music* may be seen as a forerunner of this and other iconic public sculptural projects. But only thanks to the extraordinary generosity and determination of a group of committed individuals and organisations did this major site-specific work by one of the greatest sculptors of the late twentieth century find its way onto the quayside in the town of Poole.

The fascinating story of how this happened is told here in Alastair Sooke's illuminating essay, and recalled by Caro himself in a previously unpublished note written in 1991. The reason for publishing this book now is that, after over 25 years of standing up to Poole's harsh maritime climate, *Sea Music* has been conserved and repainted and is being justly celebrated through a programme of art and heritage activities.

However, the sculpture and viewing platforms no longer look quite as they did in 1991. Shortly before he died in 2013, Caro specified that he would like all the architectural elements to be painted silver to better distinguish them from the blue of the sculpture itself. We are very pleased to have been able to carry out the artist's wishes. David Ward's photographs of *Sea Music*, taken before and after the conservation and repainting, capture these changes.

The celebration of *Sea Music* has involved multiple art forms, and we are pleased that Jim Aitchison composed a new work for the Bournemouth Symphony Orchestra to perform at the relaunch, again by Lord Palumbo, on 13 May 2017. The composer describes here how his composition was created. At the core of Poole Museum's arts programme are exhibitions of Caro's Concerto series and of Ward's photographs, as well as Caro's *Slow March* (1985) sited outside the museum. In his essay Stephen Feeke describes how the whole conservation and celebration programme – a partnership once again of a range of organisations and individuals – came about and contextualises *Sea Music* within Caro's career.

We are grateful to all those who have contributed to the programme, but from a long list I would like to select a few for special mention. Paul Caro and Patrick Cunningham of Barford Sculptures have been immensely supportive of our project from its inception. They asked Madeleine Bessborough and Stephen Feeke of the New Art Centre, Roche Court, and Emma Kerr of the Roche Court Educational Trust if they would work closely with us to make it happen, and they have indeed been excellent project partners. Tom Roberts, designer of the viewing platforms, has again been involved, helping us with the conservation project.

Thanks also go to Michael Armstrong of SoundStorm Music Education Agency and to the many artists involved with the programme, including Jim Aitchison, David Ward and Jonathan Parsons; Lisa Tregale at the Bournemouth Symphony

Orchestra; and Pavilion Dance South West and the staff and students at Bournemouth and Poole College.

Several members of the Poole Museum team have been engaged with the project, but I must single out for thanks our *Sea Music* project manager, Melinda McCheyne, our Borough of Poole surveyor and project manager, John Kerley, and our wonderful team of volunteers from Culture Volunteers Poole. We are also enormously grateful to the community of people who were involved with the original project, or have decided to support it now, and have given time, reminiscences and new insights.

Finally, the whole programme would not have been possible without significant funding from a number of benefactors and organisations, most notably the Heritage Lottery Fund and Arts Council England. Conserving modern sculpture might on the face of it be thought of as an unusual activity for the Heritage Lottery Fund, but *Sea Music* is an important element of Poole's heritage, and I thank the HLF South West committee members and staff for their vision in supporting the project. We are also very grateful to Suzanne Deal Booth and David and Audrey Mirvish for supporting *Sea of Music* by Jim Aitchison and additional thanks are due to the Henry Moore Foundation for funding a lecture series organised with the Arts University Bournemouth.

Why have so many gone to so much trouble? The reason is that despite its art-historical importance, elegance and value in place-shaping, *Sea Music* has for too long been an underappreciated – or, by some, unloved – masterpiece, featuring only very occasionally in surveys of modern public sculpture. Now, conserved and looking magnificent, *Sea Music* can take its rightful place within Caro's legacy and as a major cultural asset of Poole's and Poole Museum's public offering.

One Hundred Views of Sea Music

Photographs by David Ward

Specially commissioned photographs of *Sea Music* arranged after, during and before restoration.

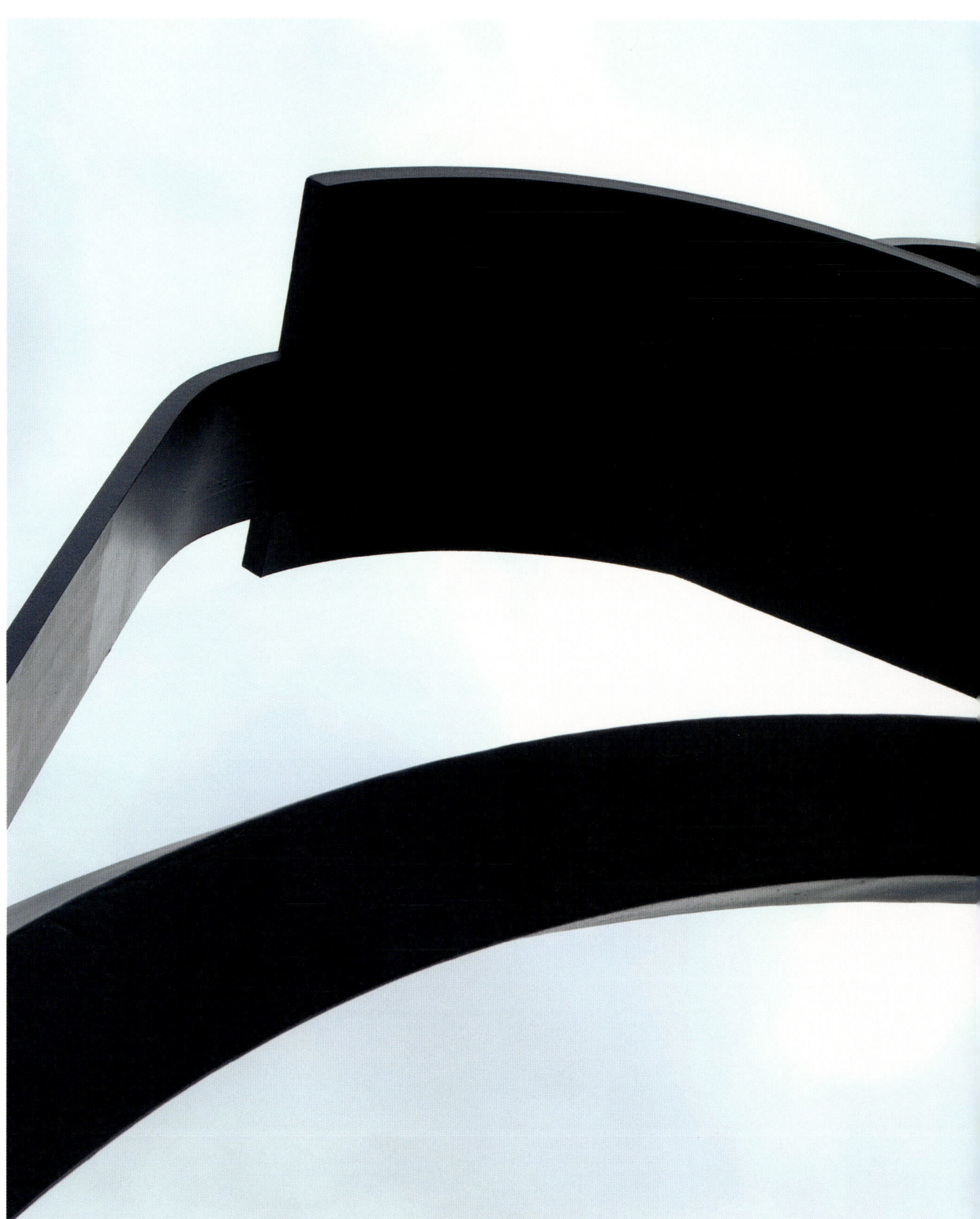

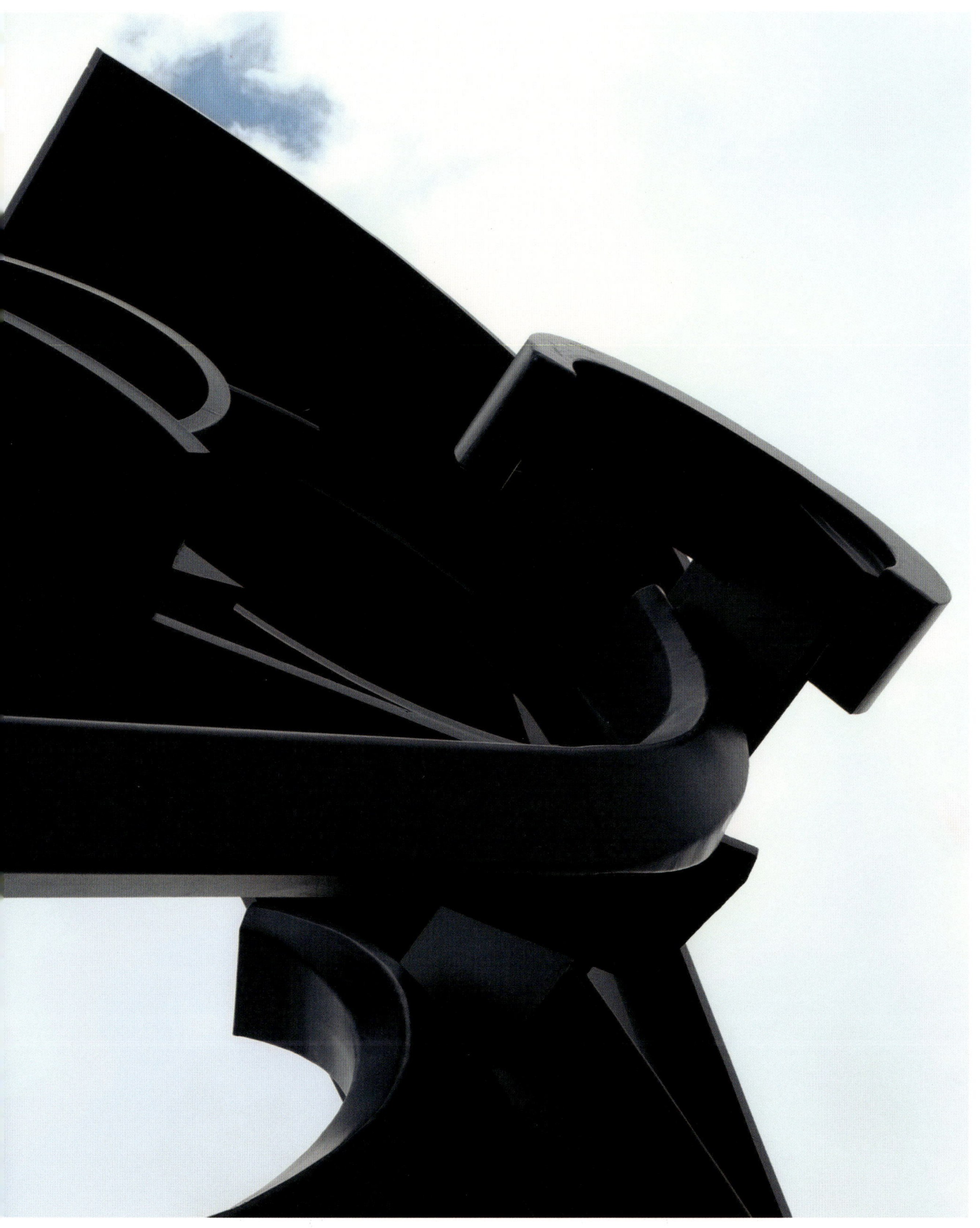

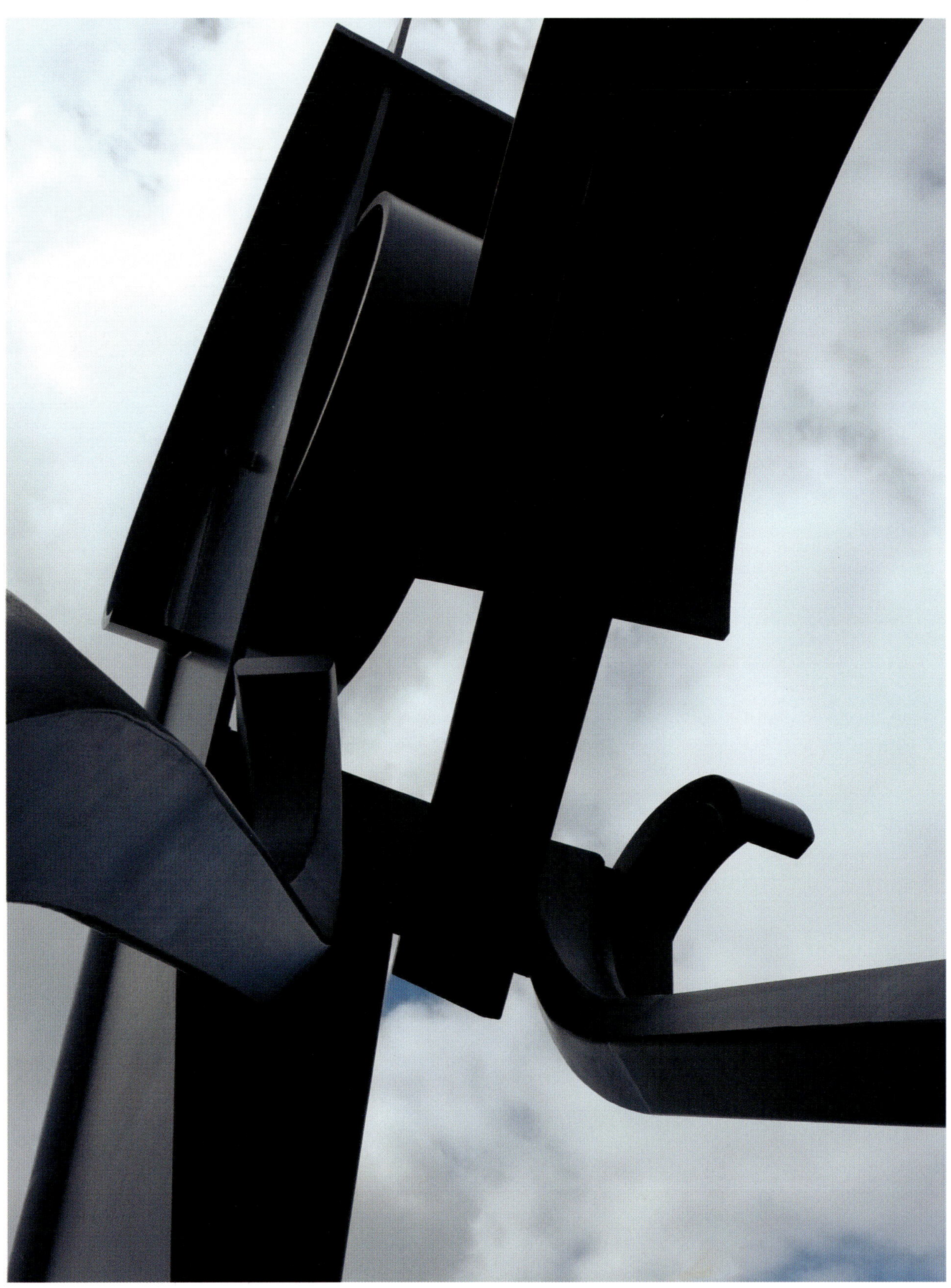

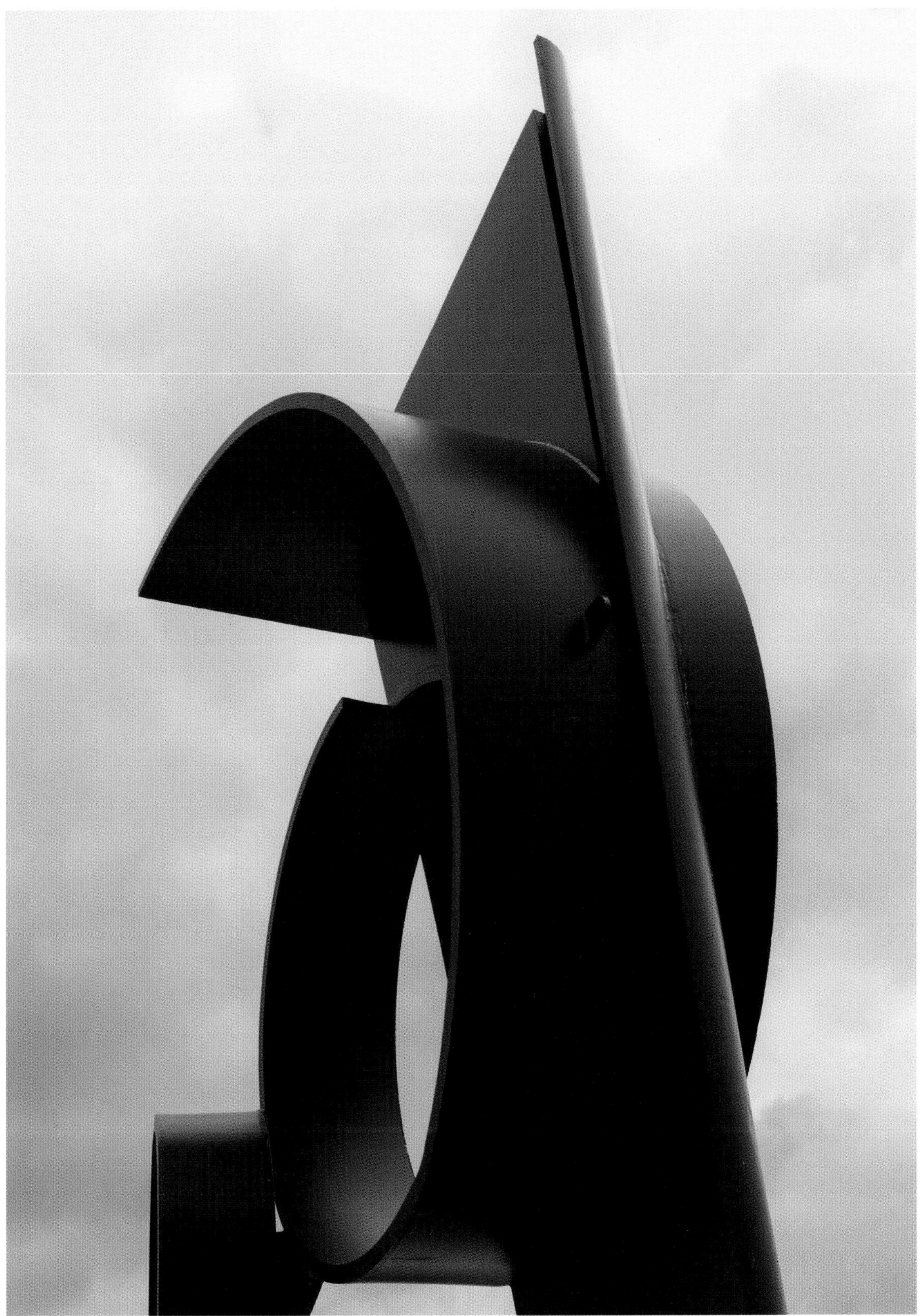

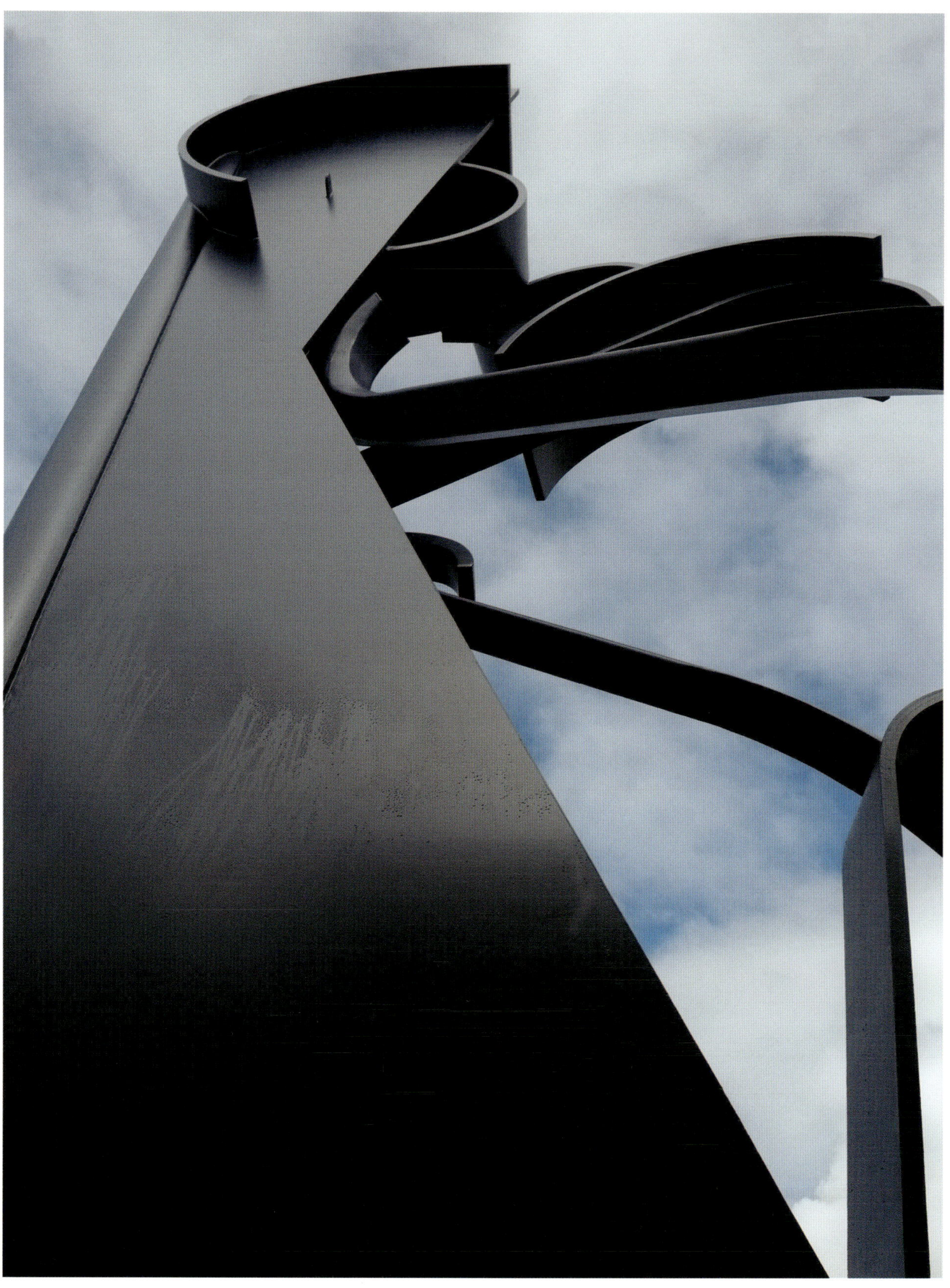

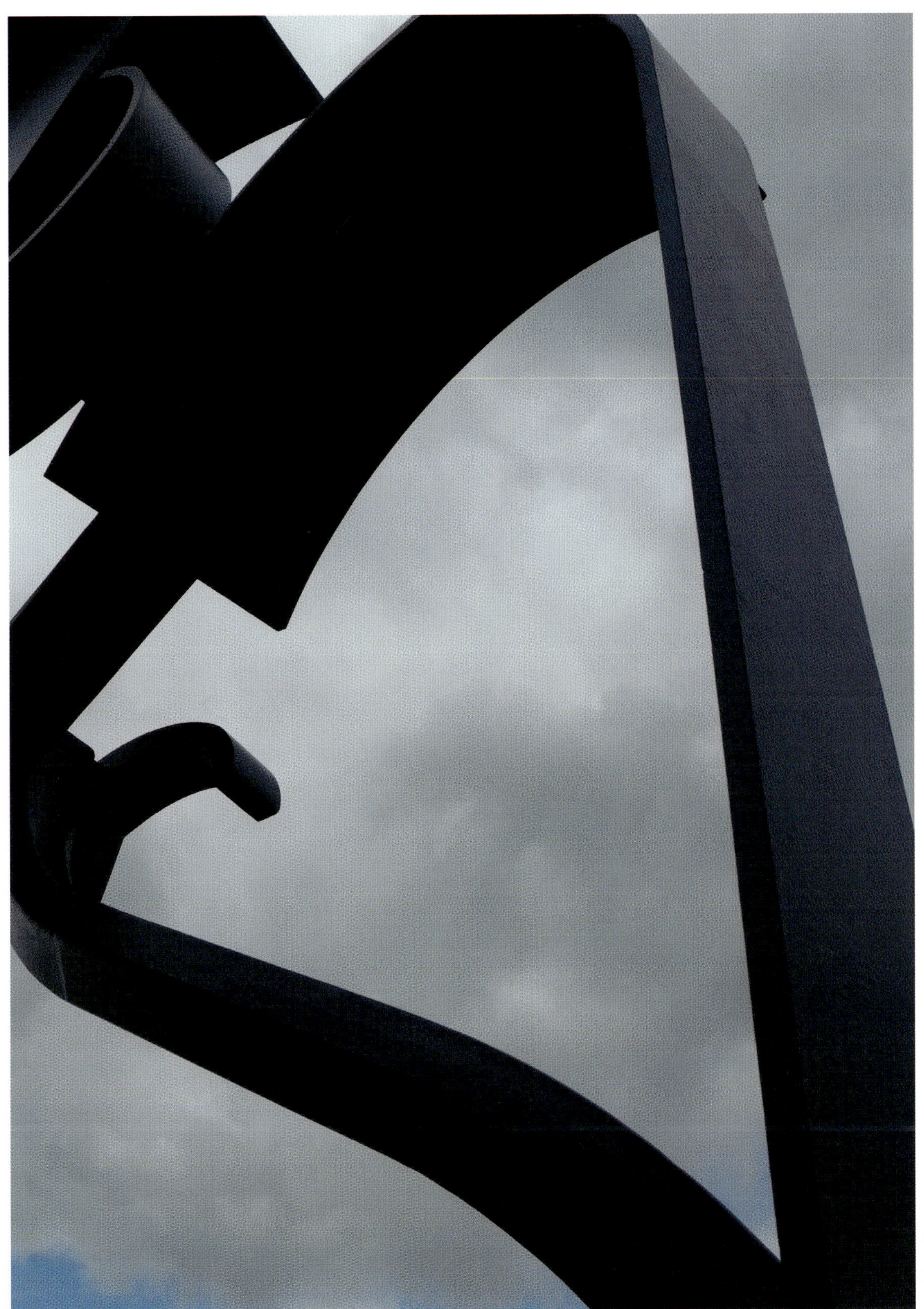

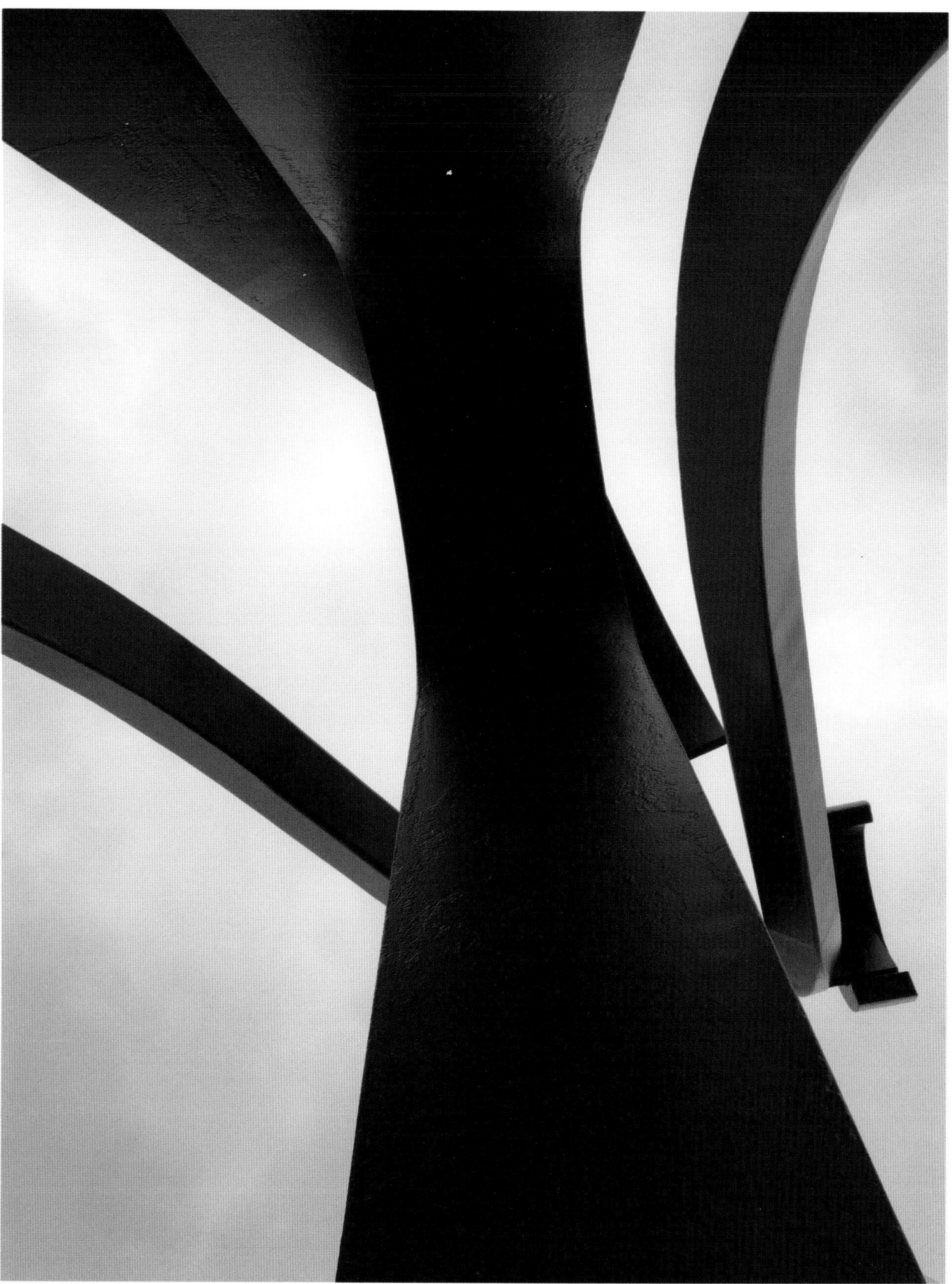

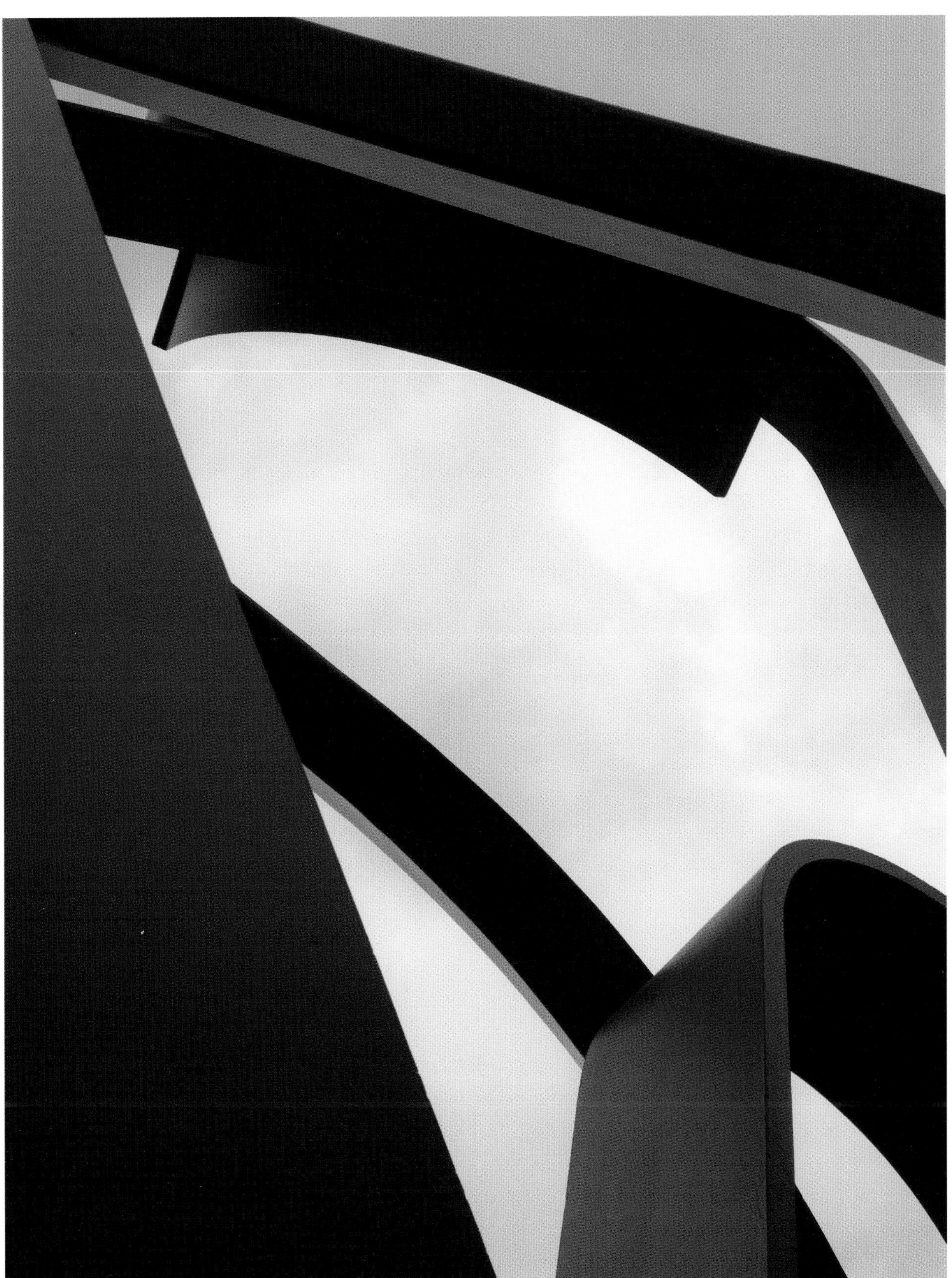

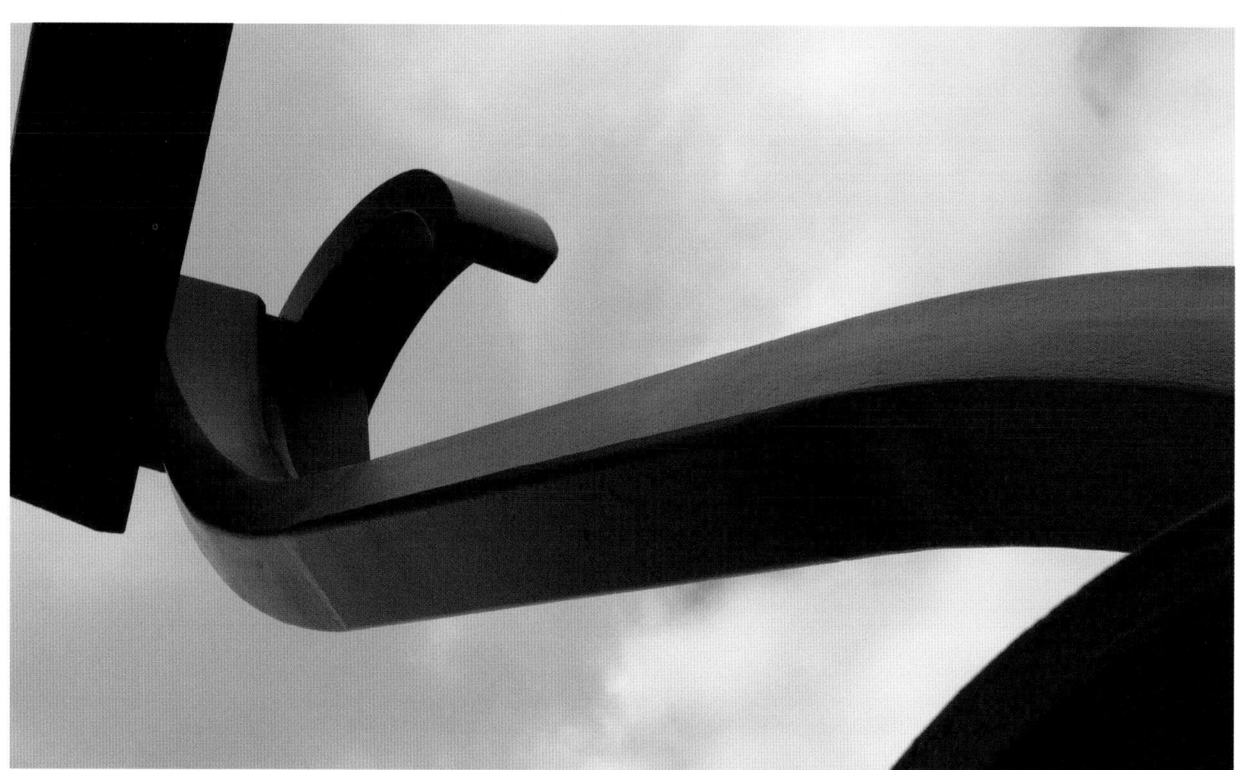

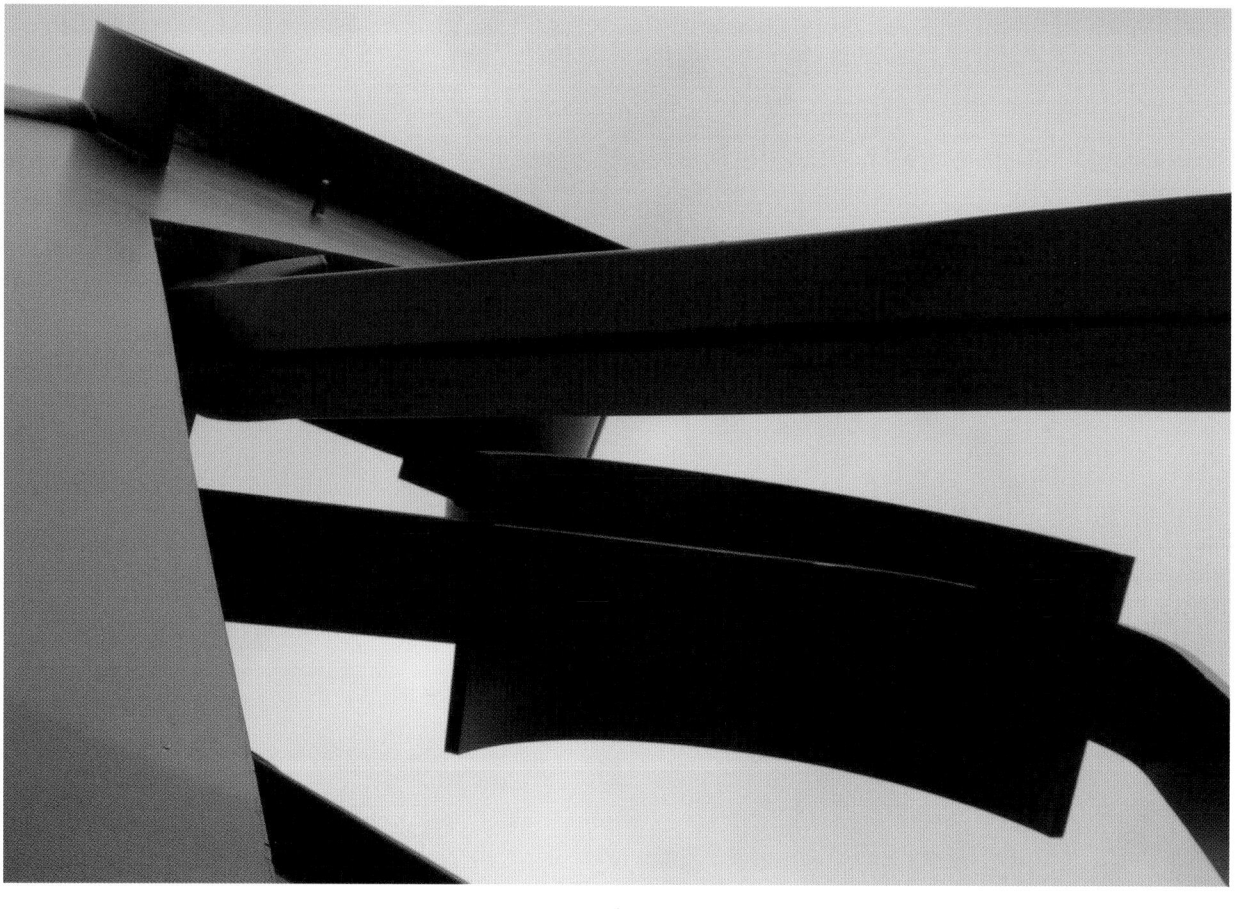

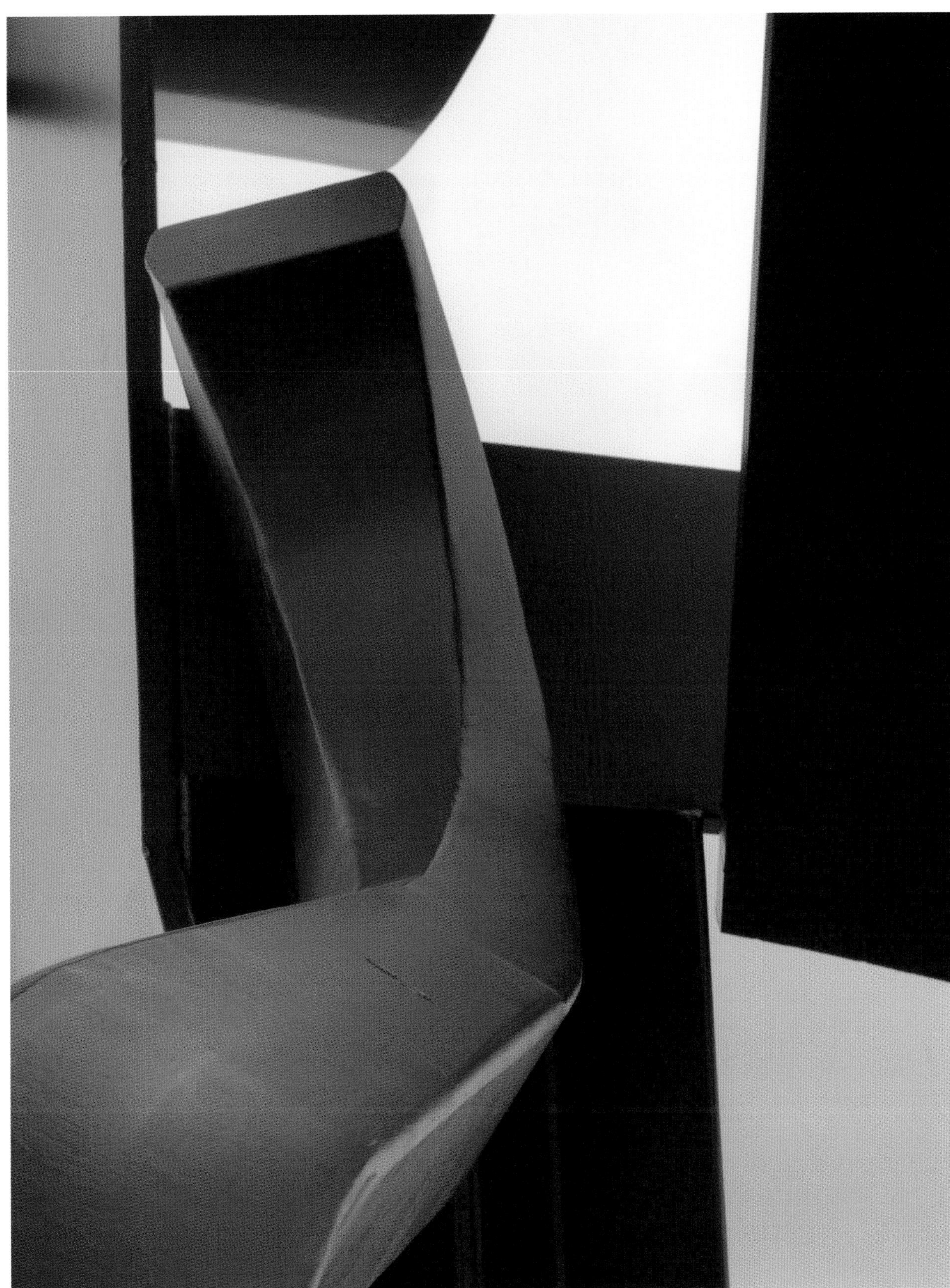

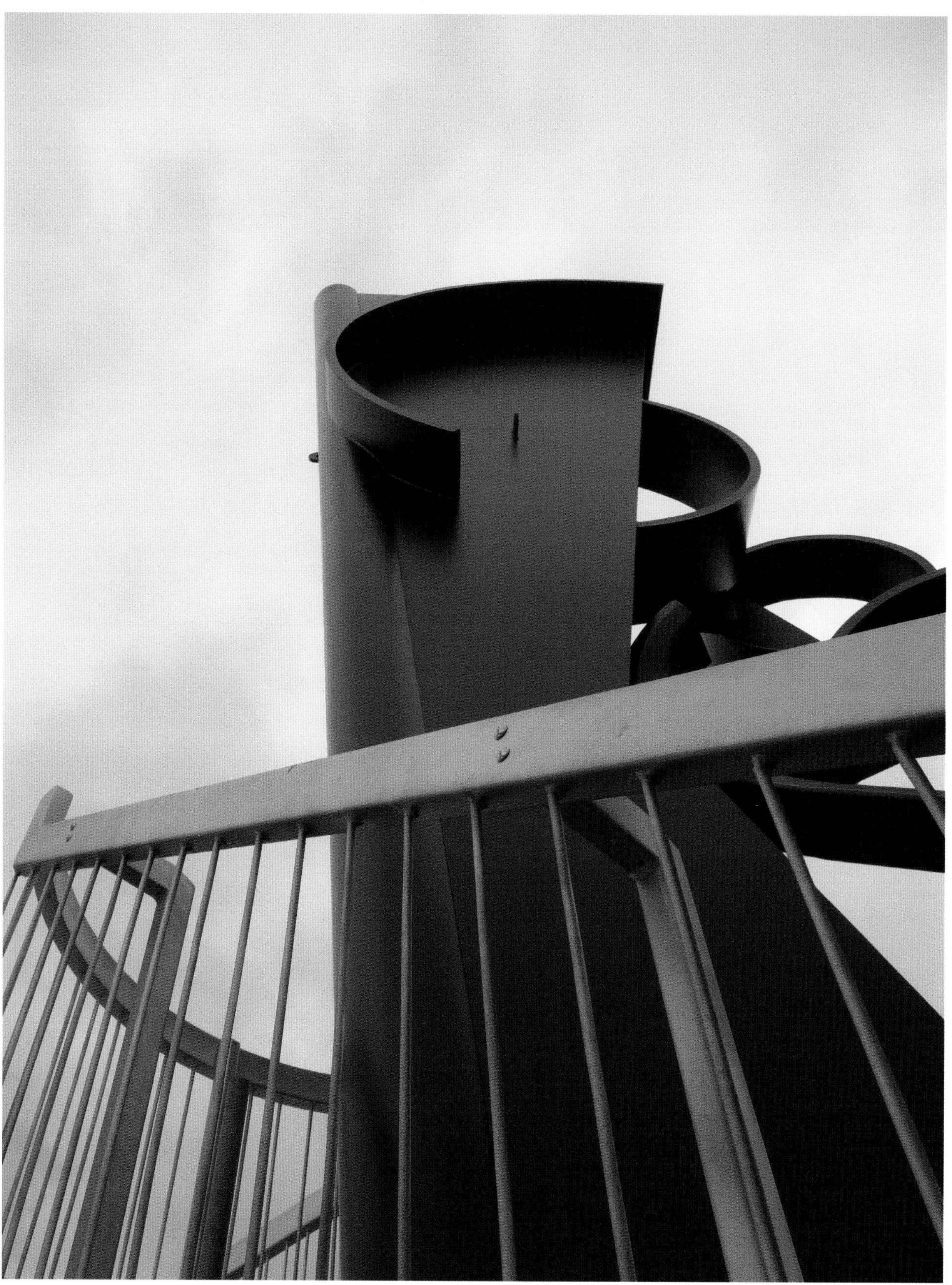

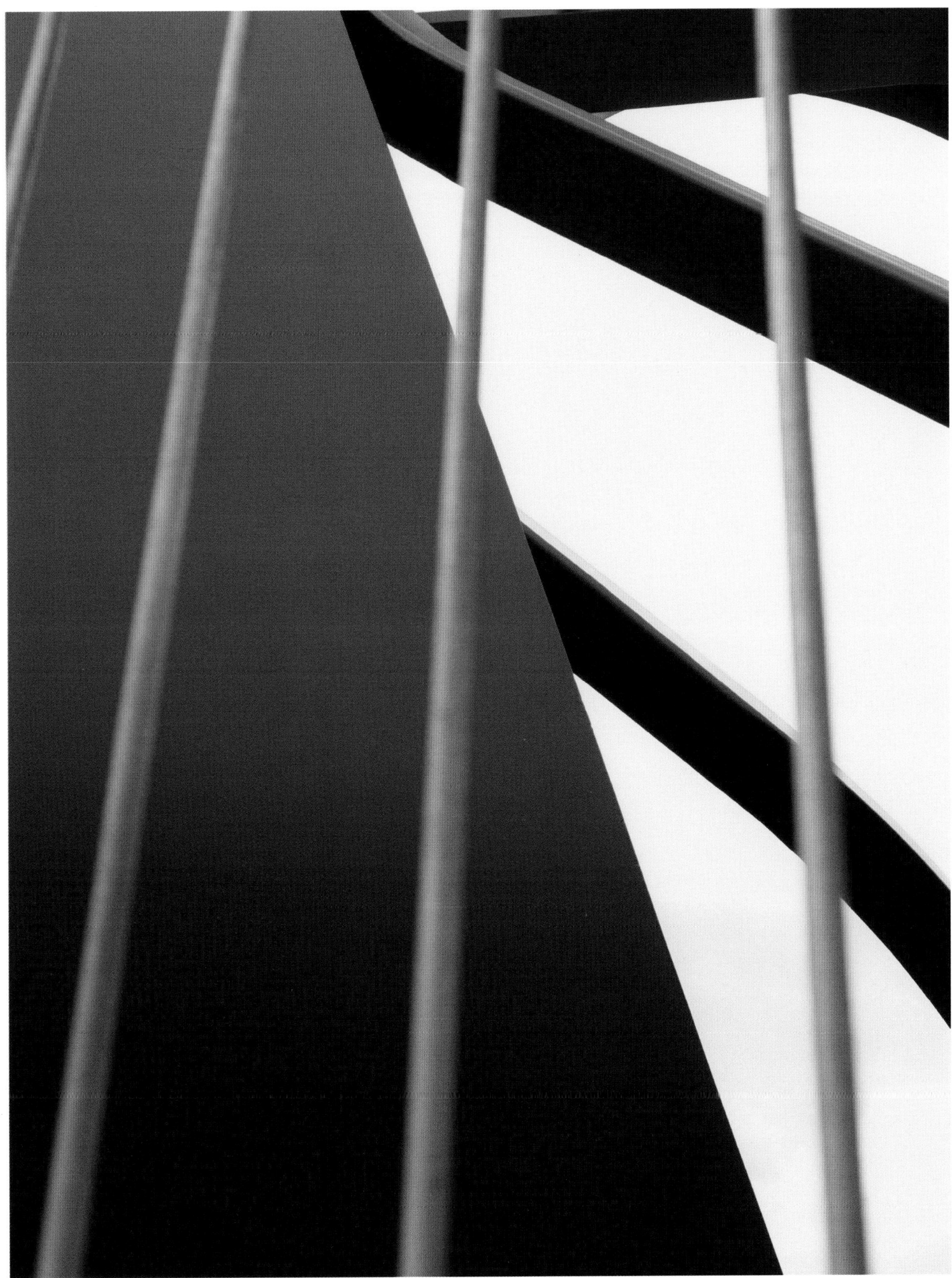

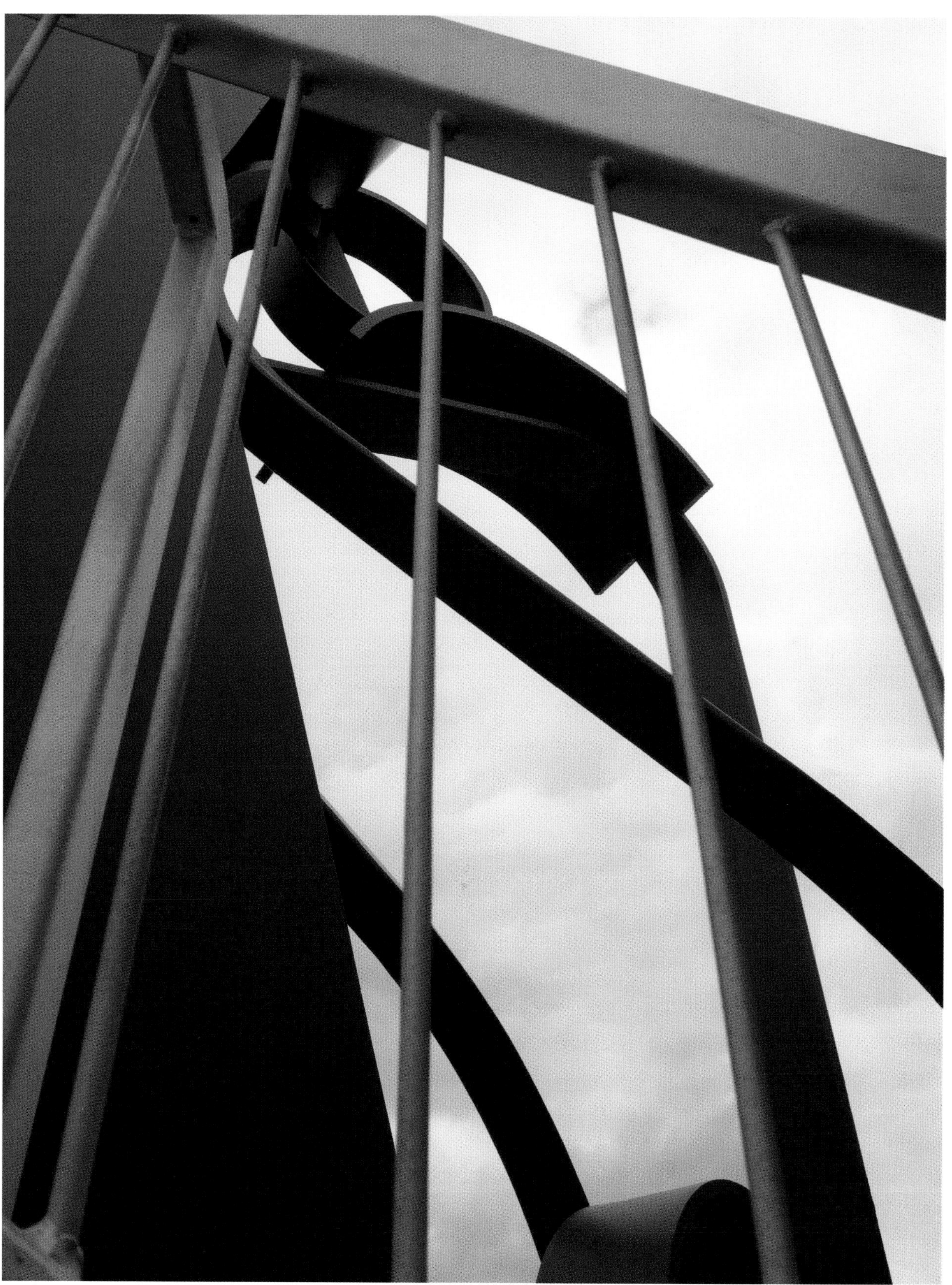

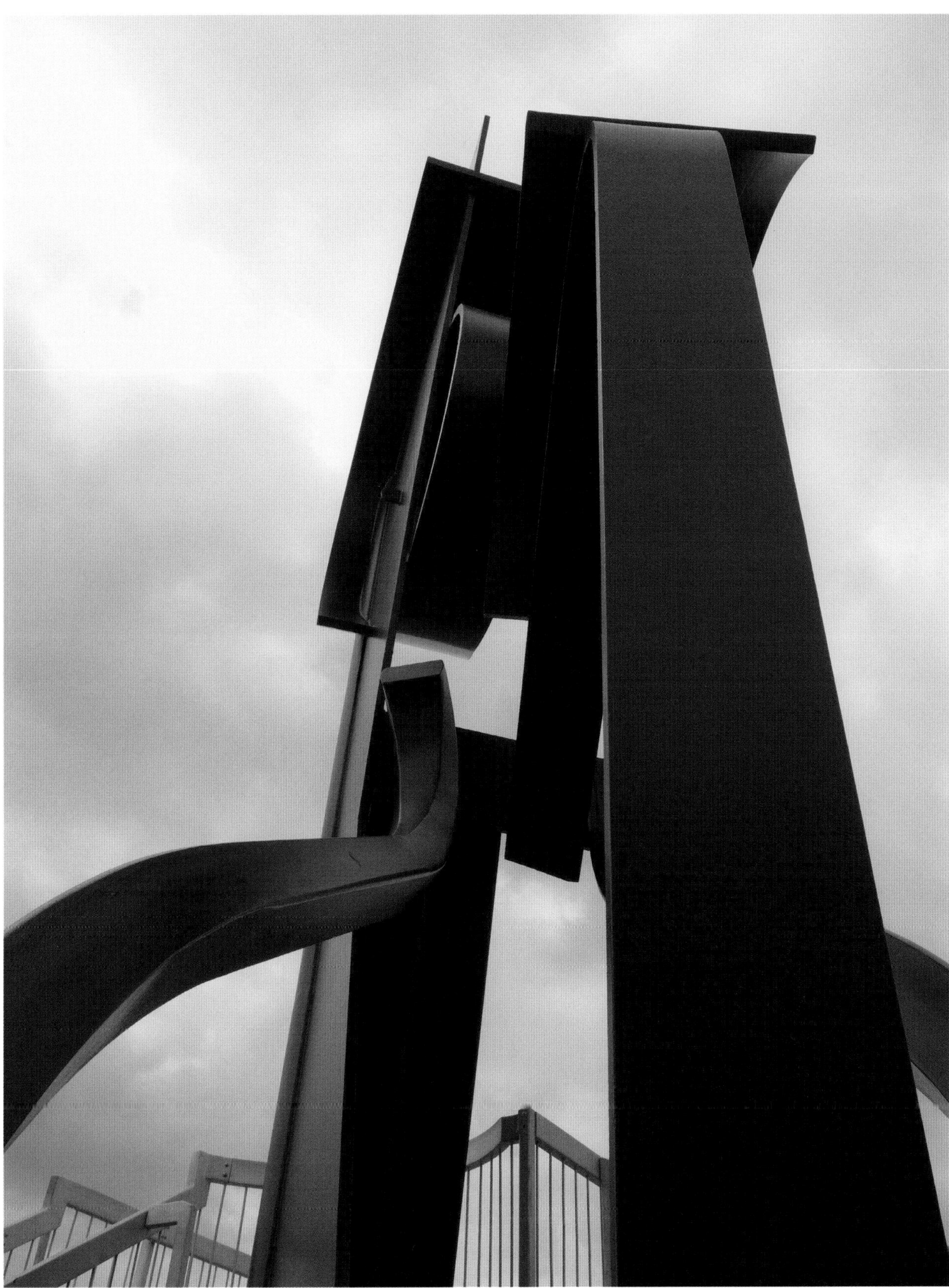

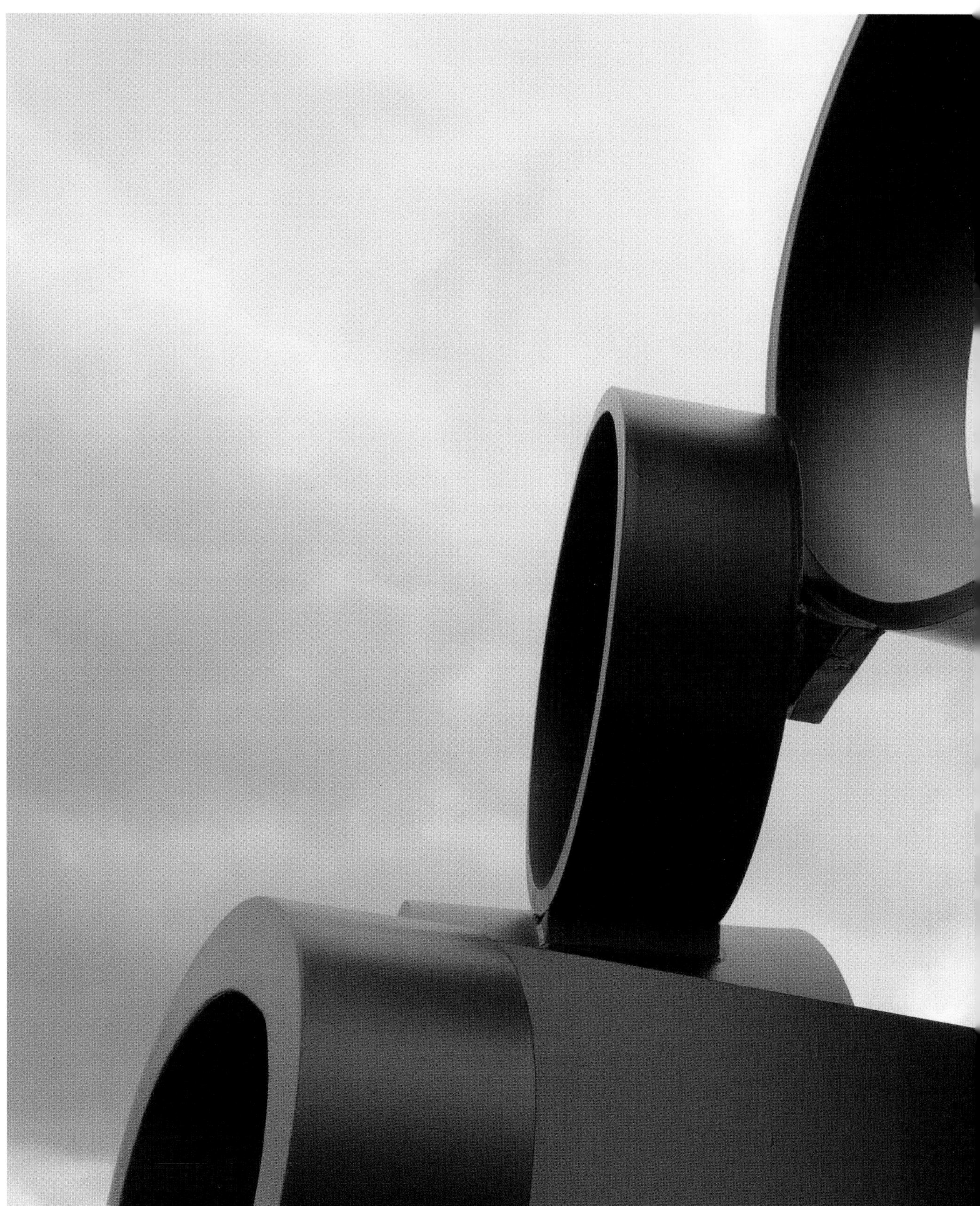

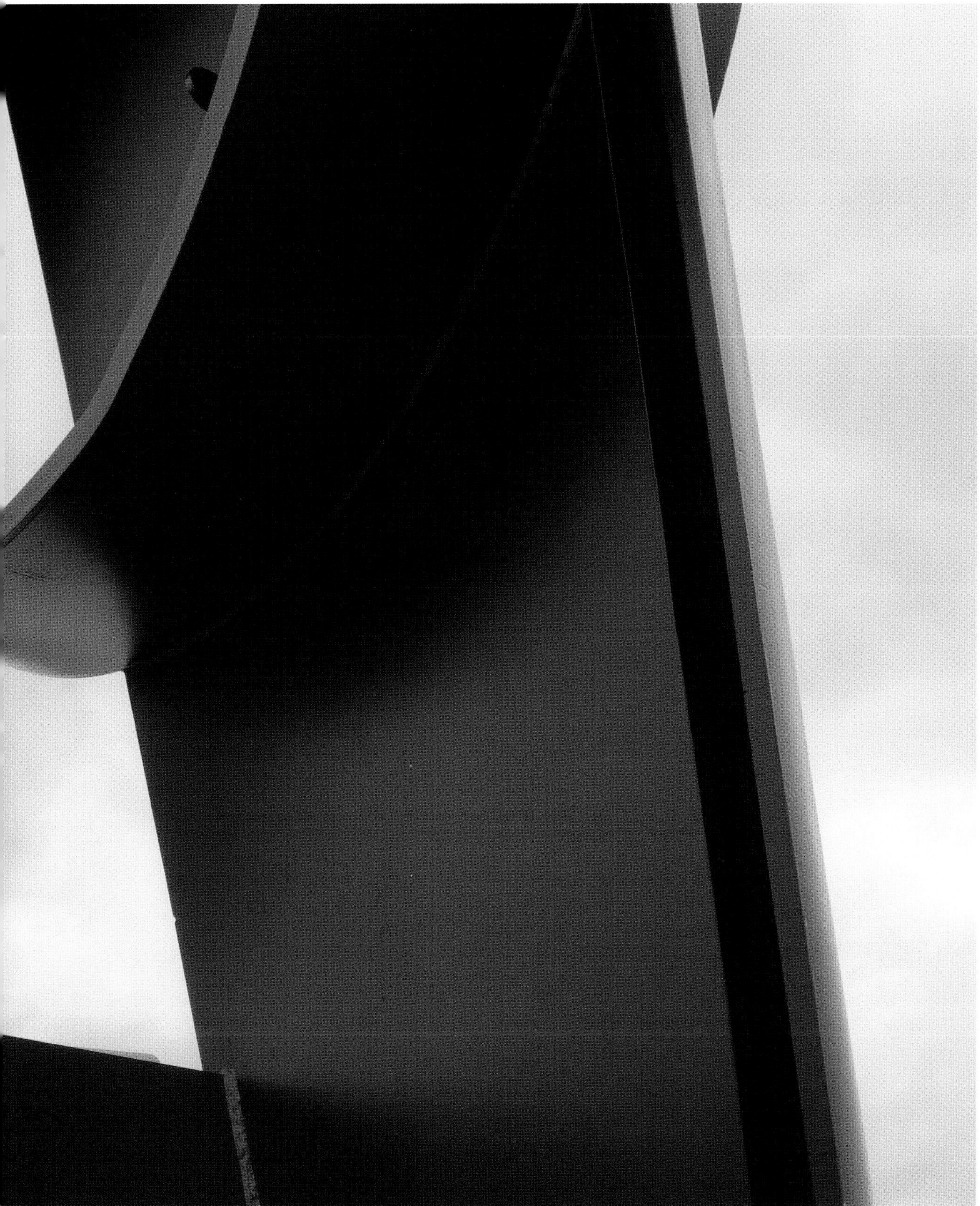

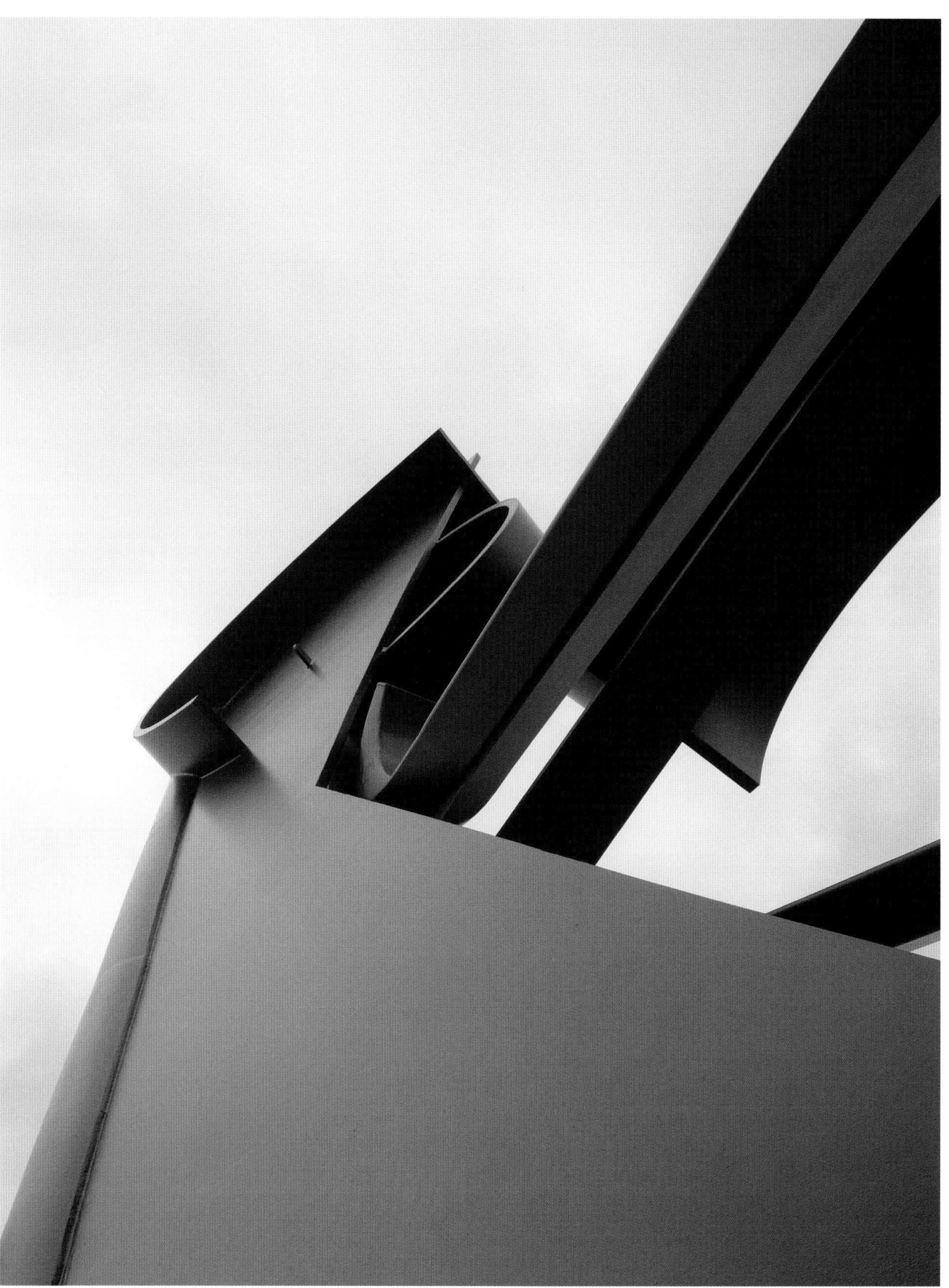

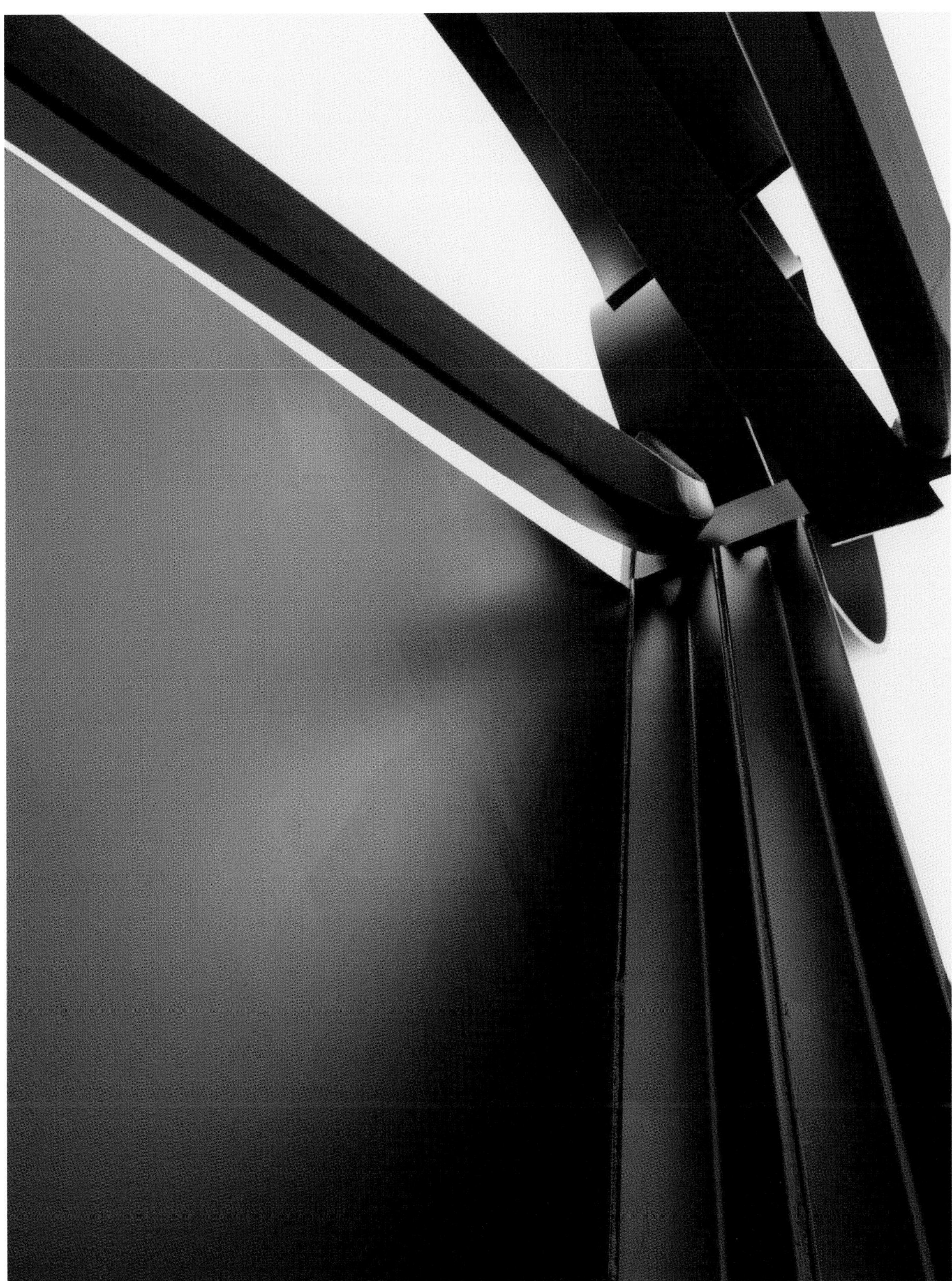

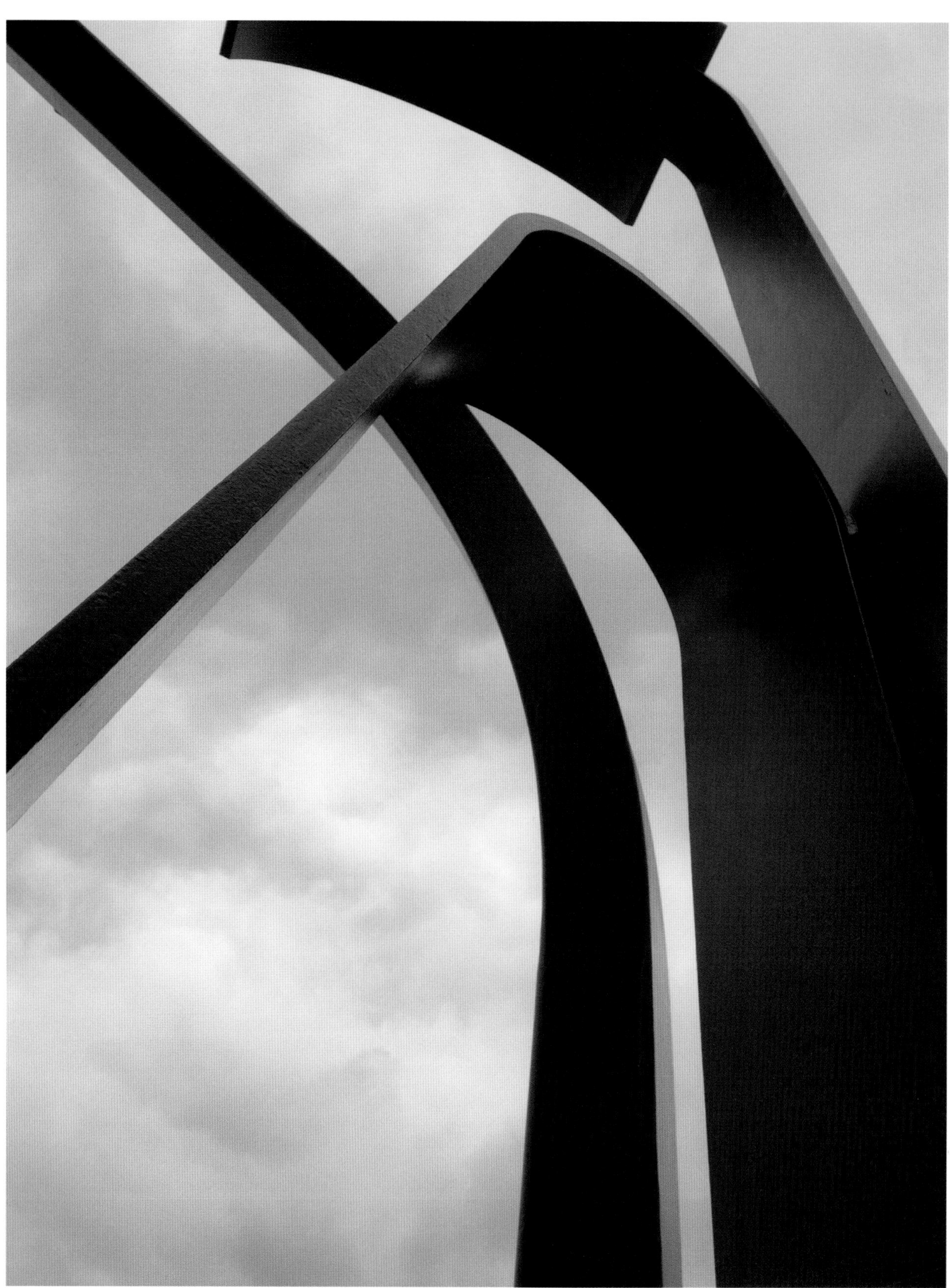

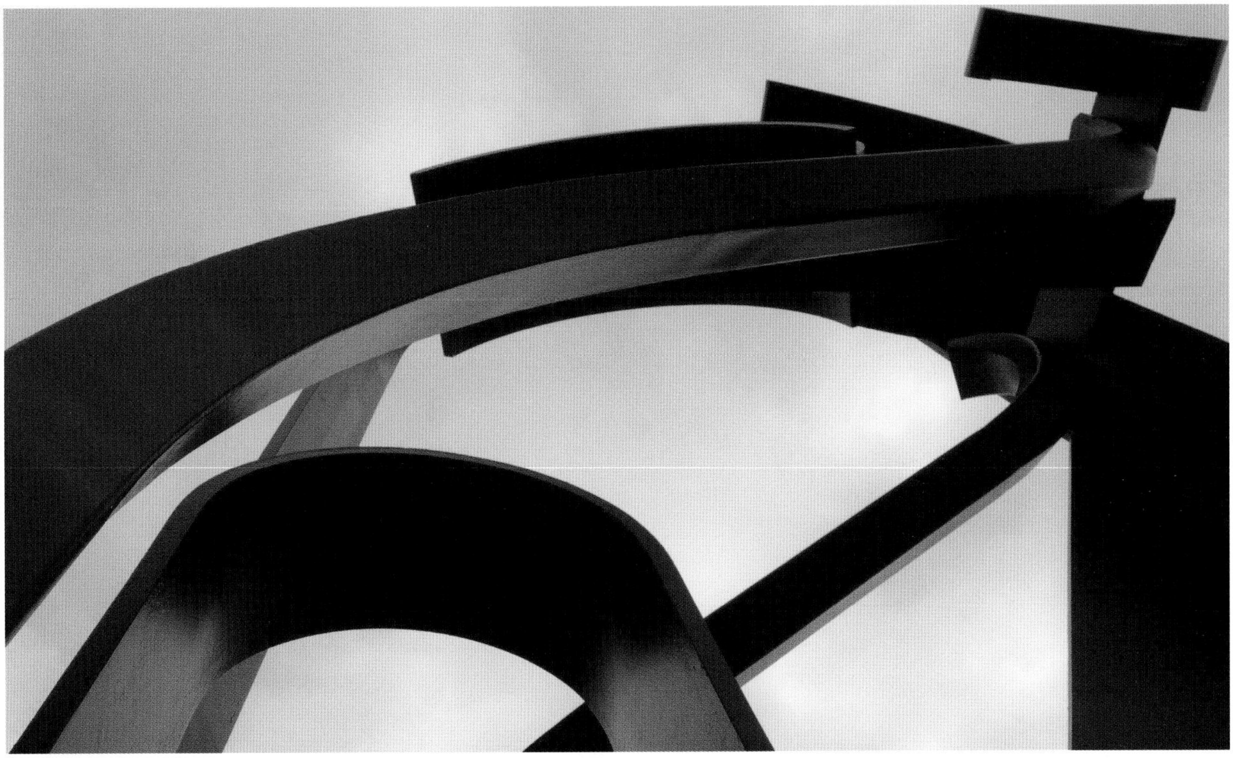

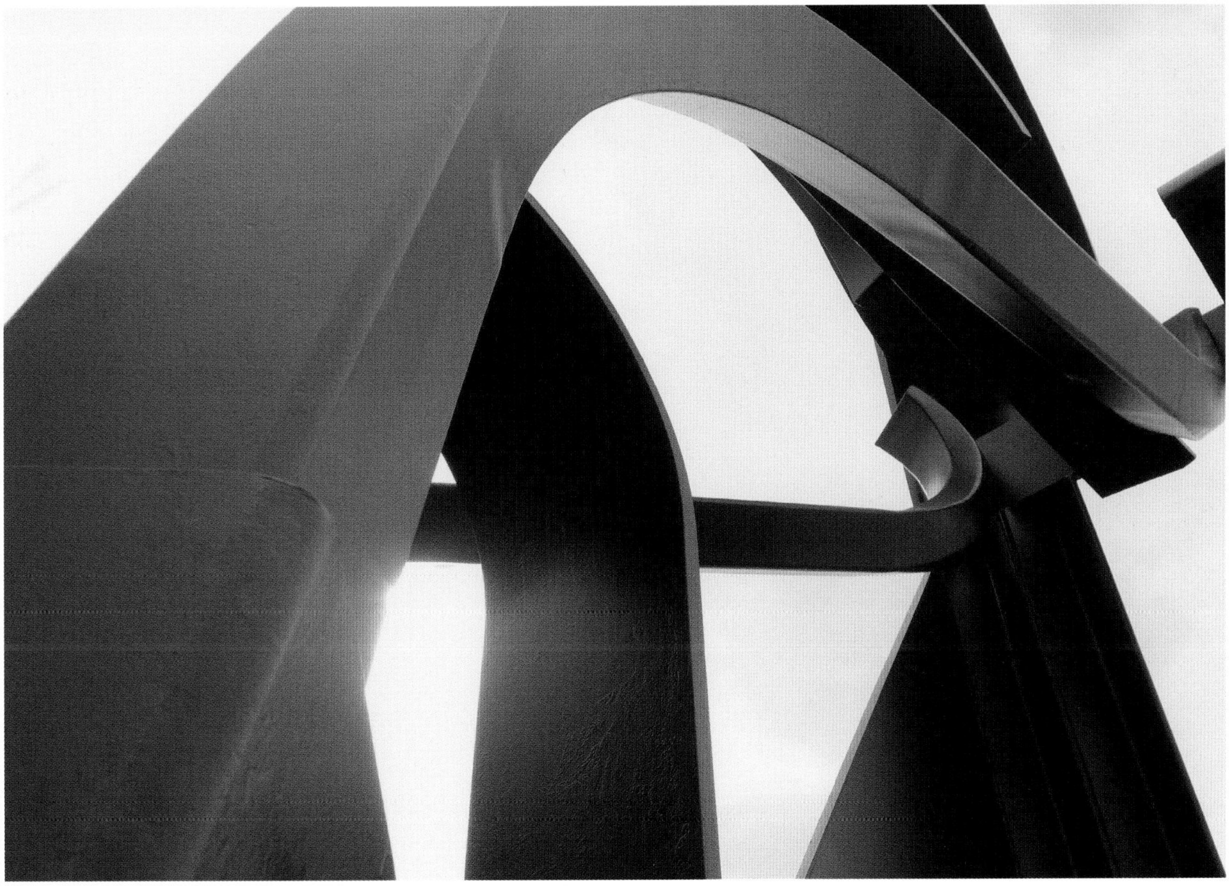

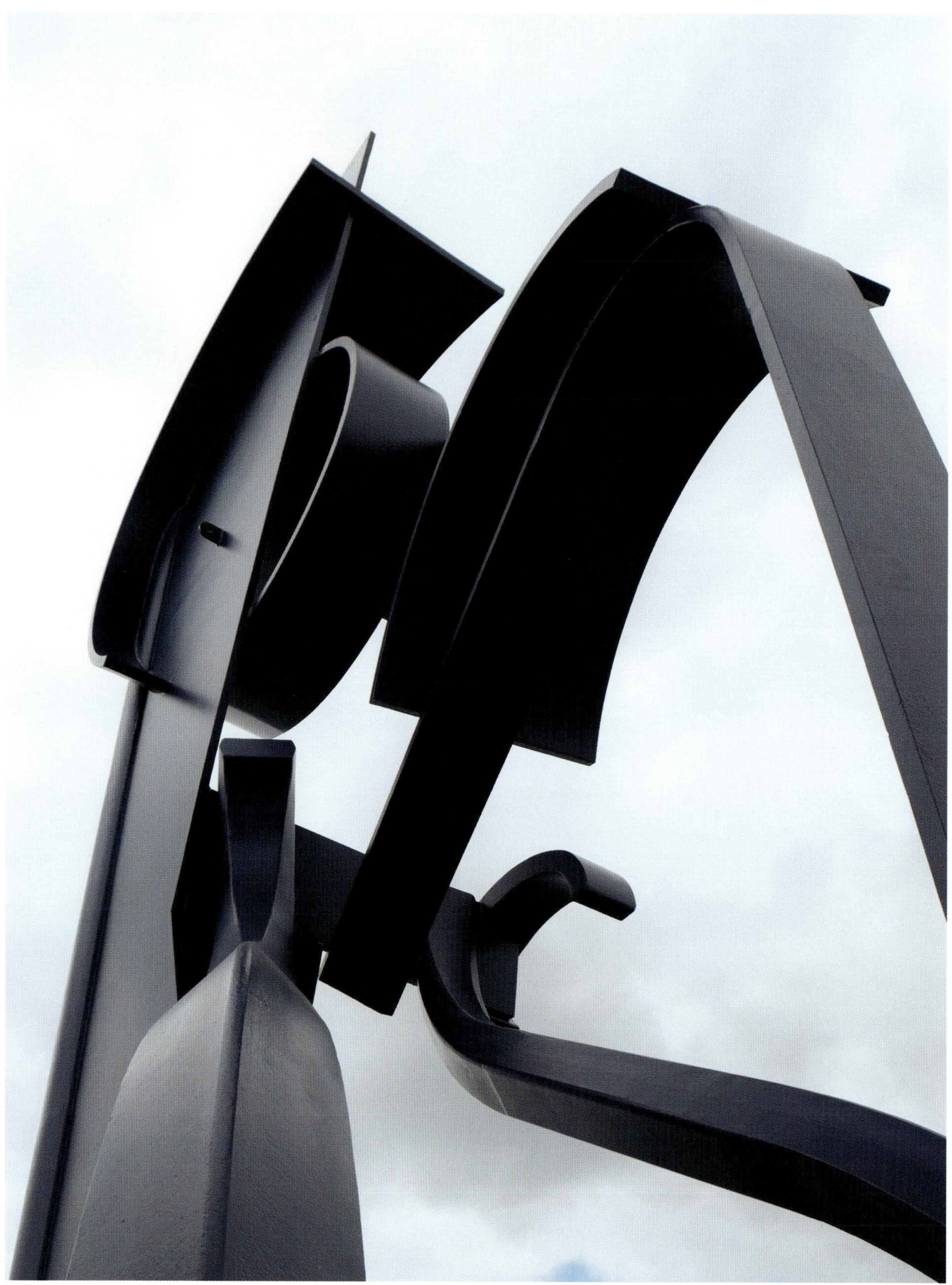

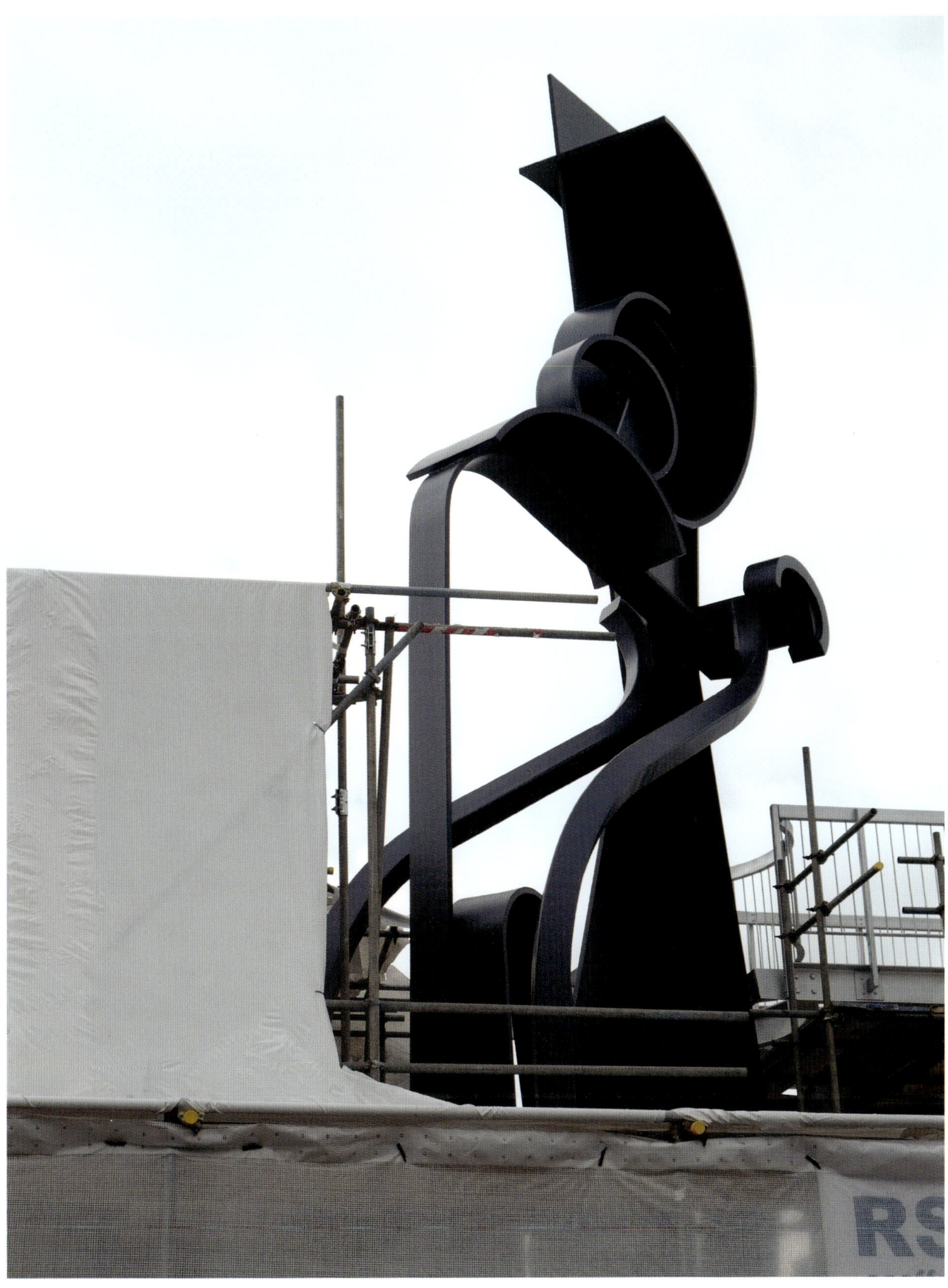

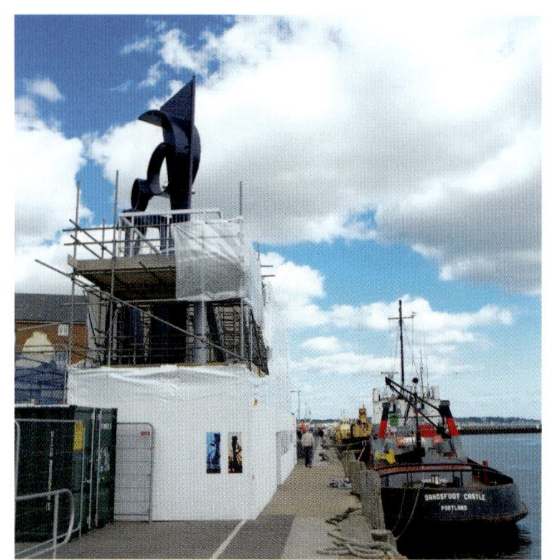
SANDSFOOT CASTLE
PORTLAND

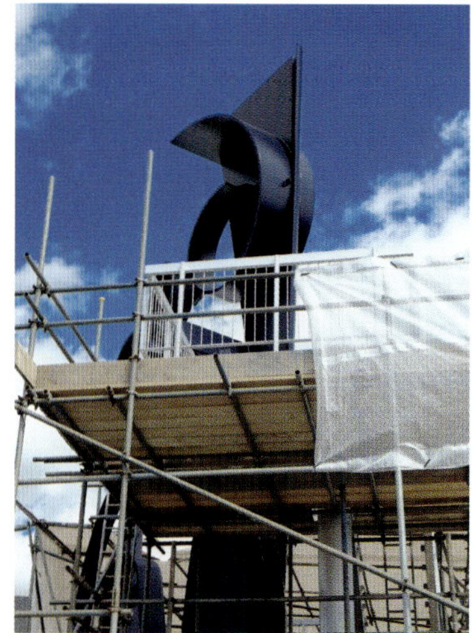

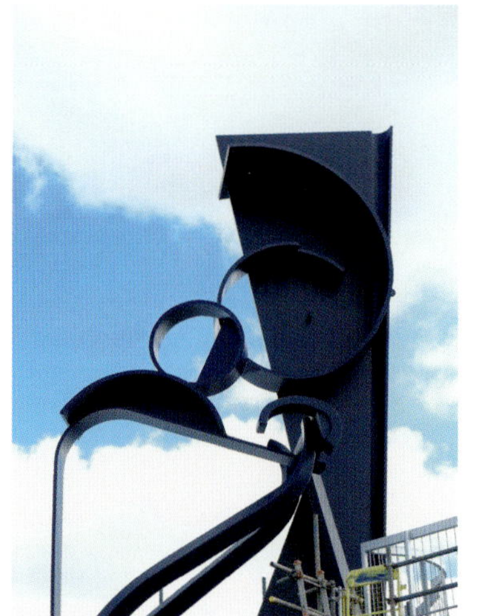

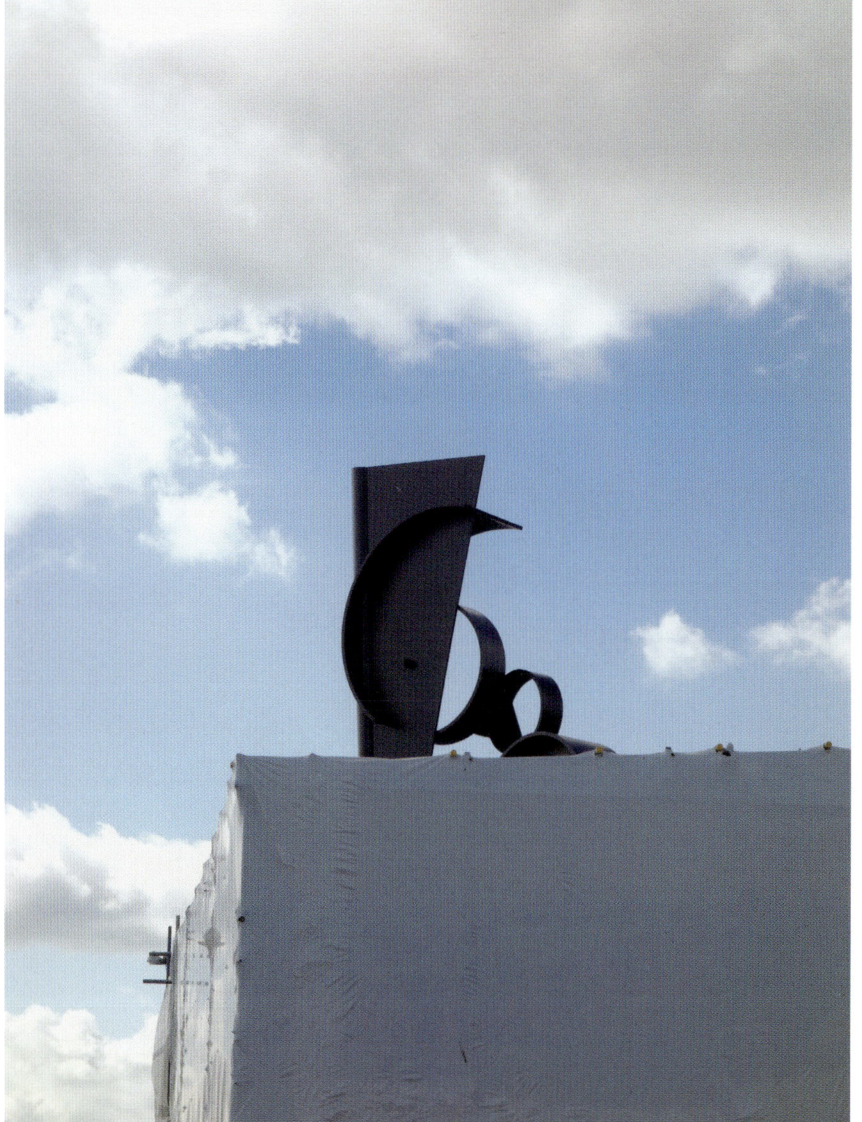

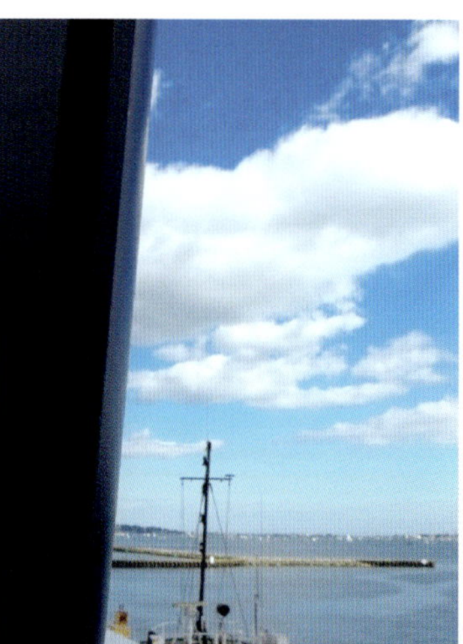

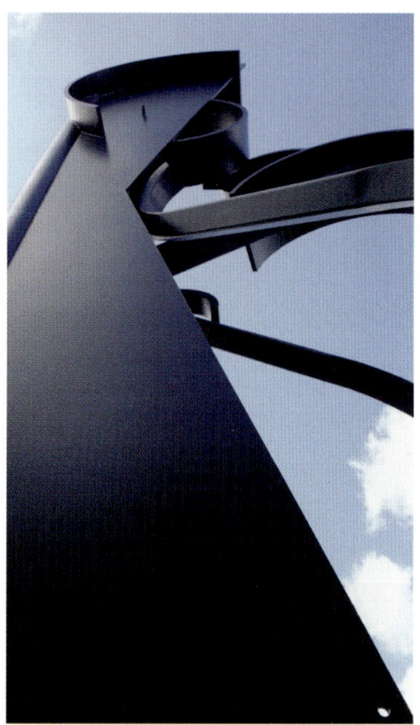

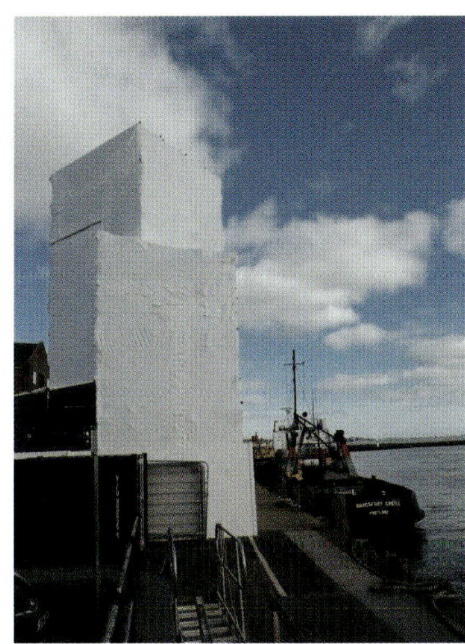

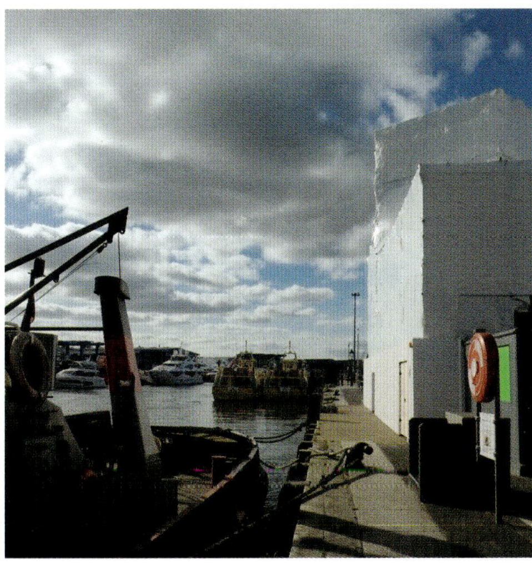

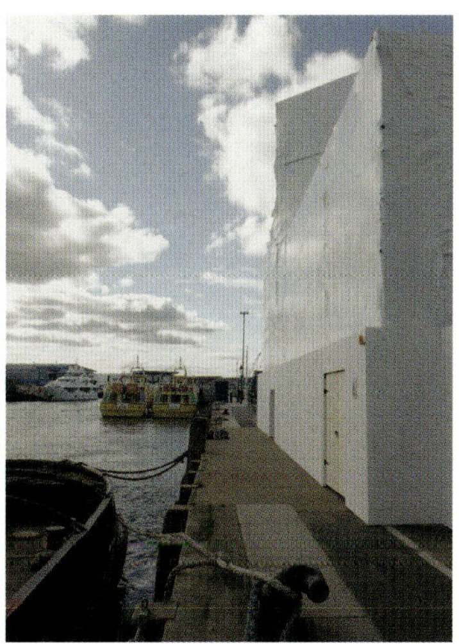

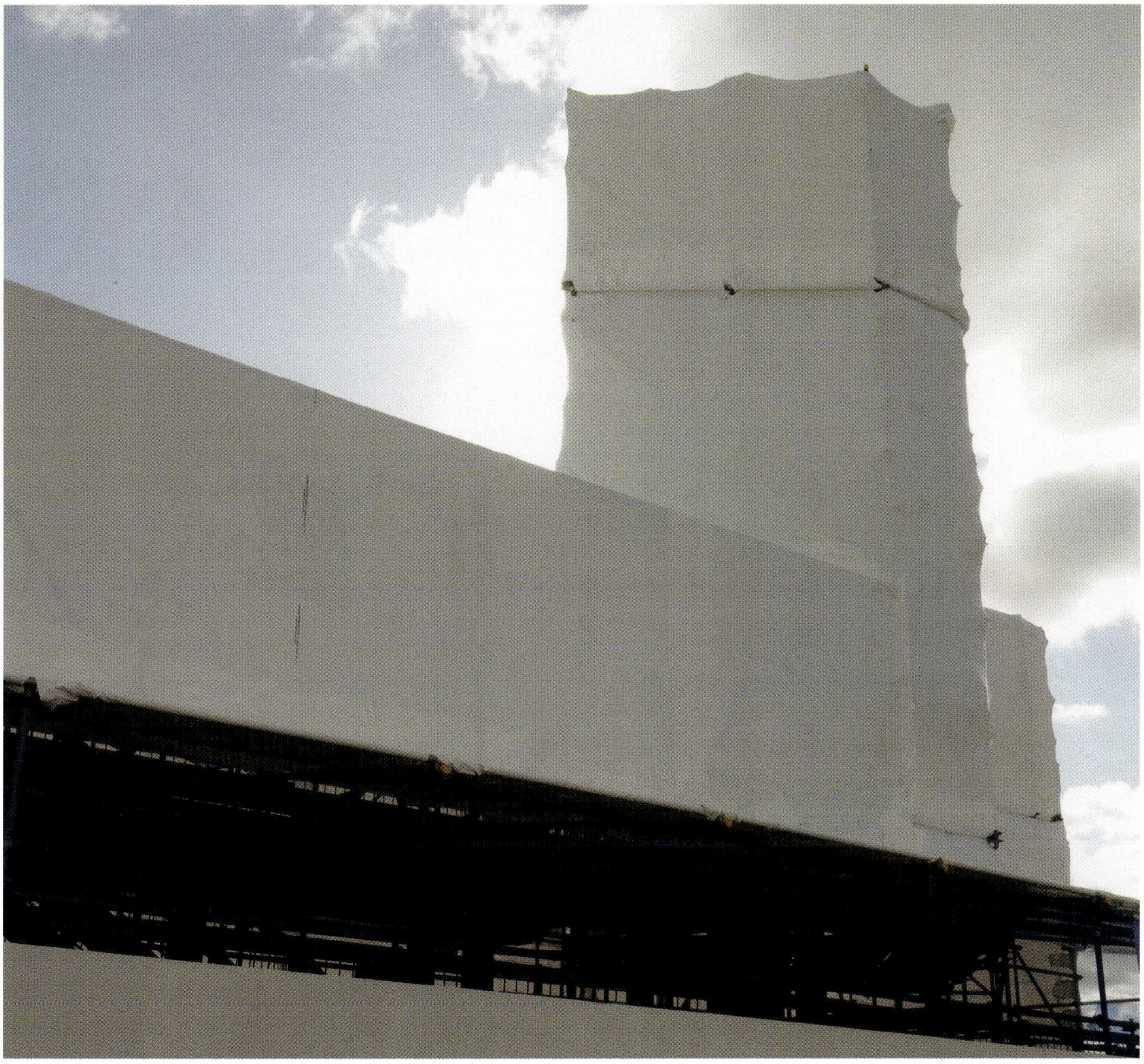

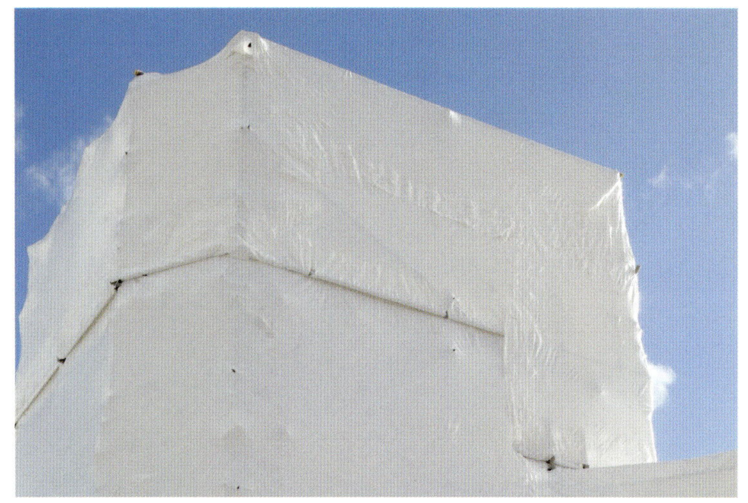

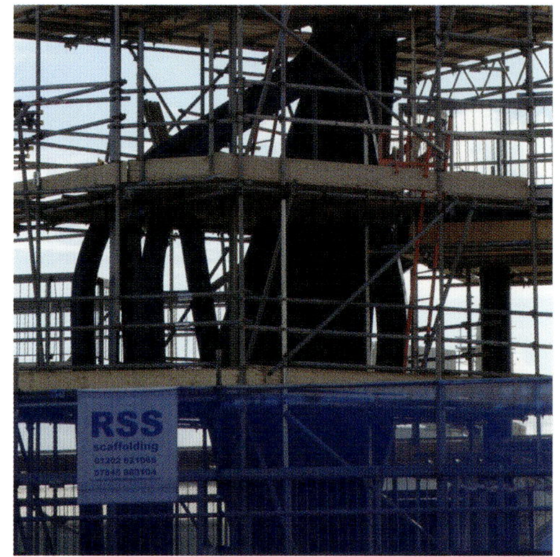
RSS
scaffolding

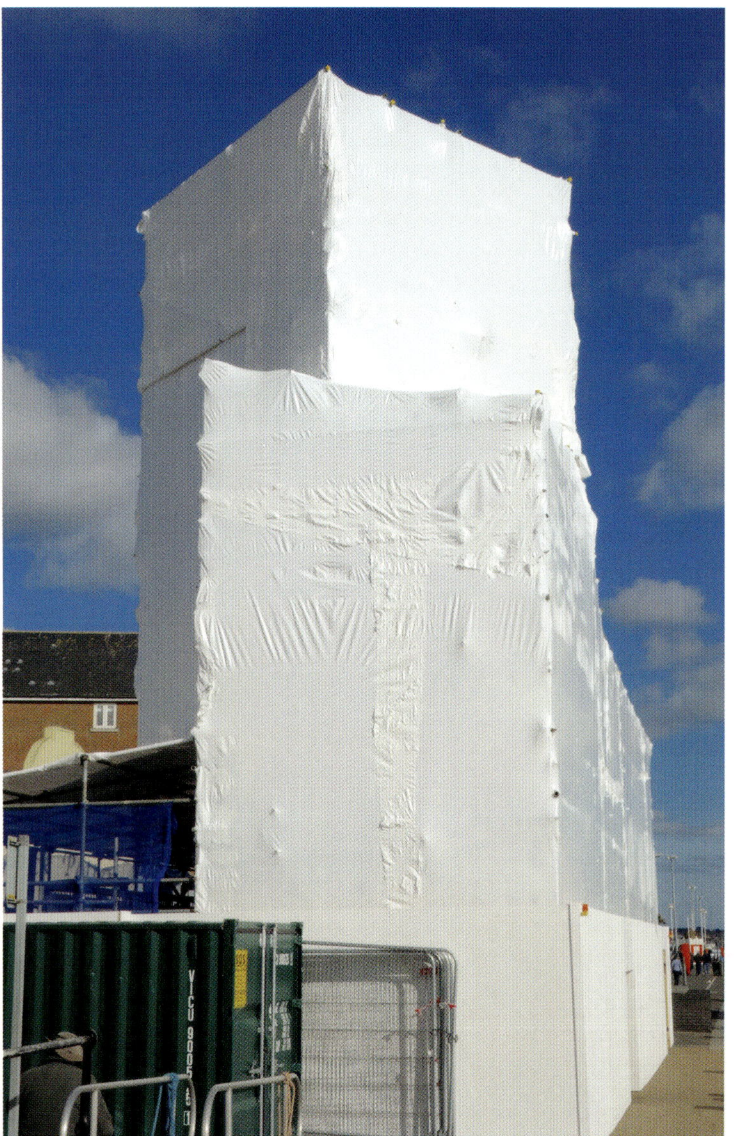

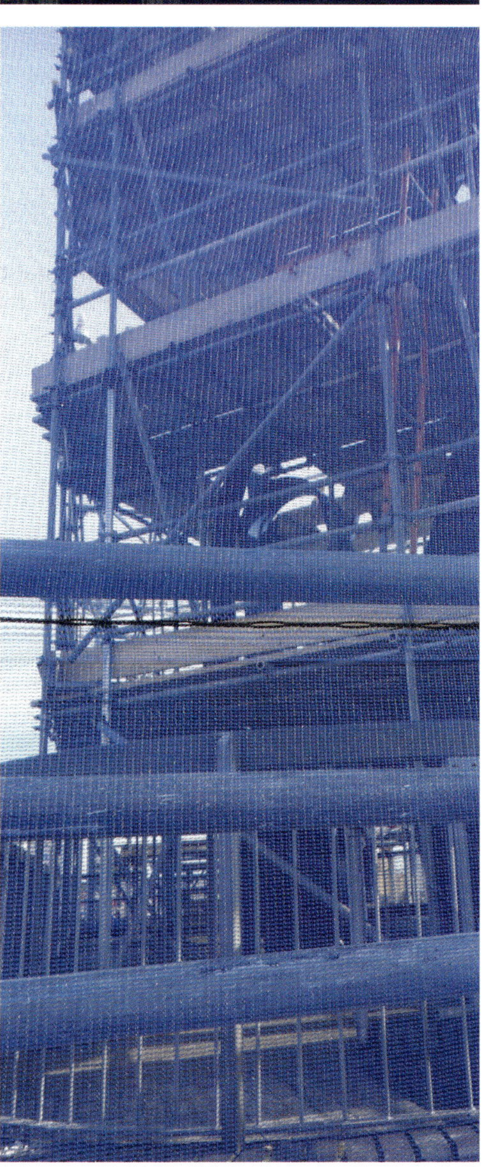

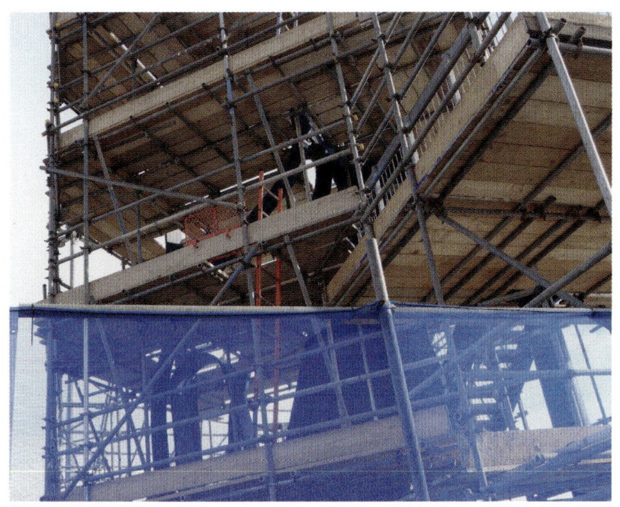

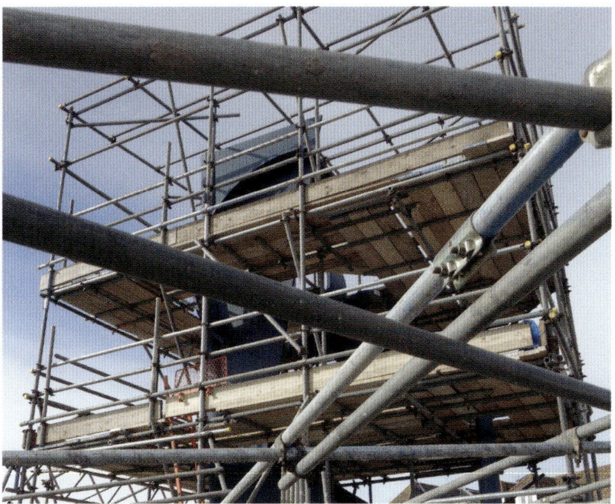

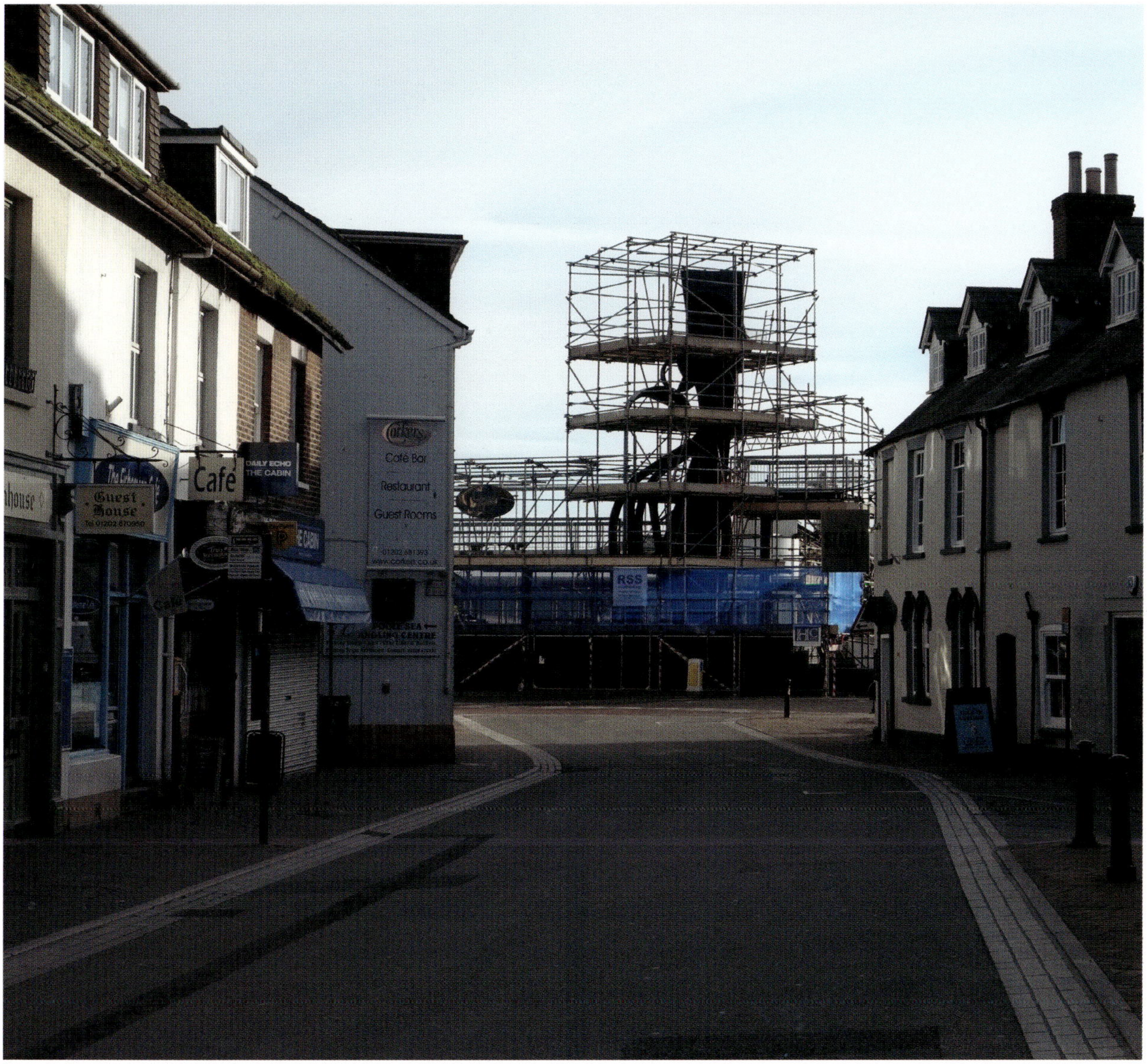

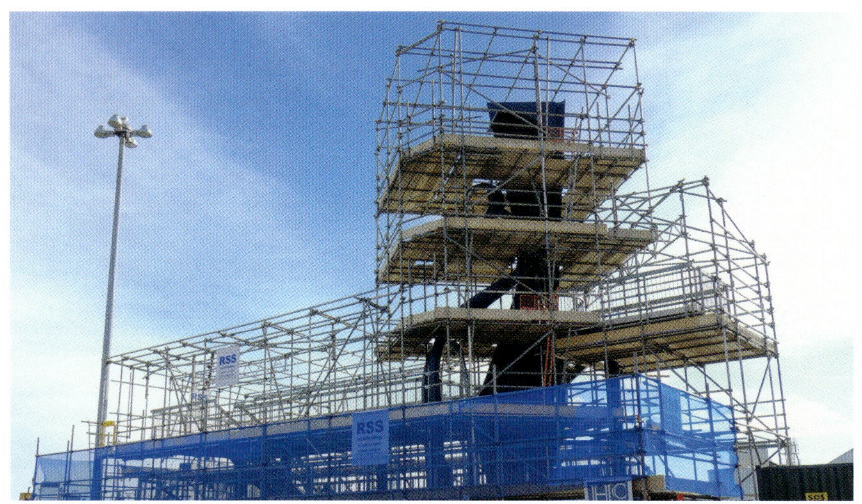
RSS
RSS

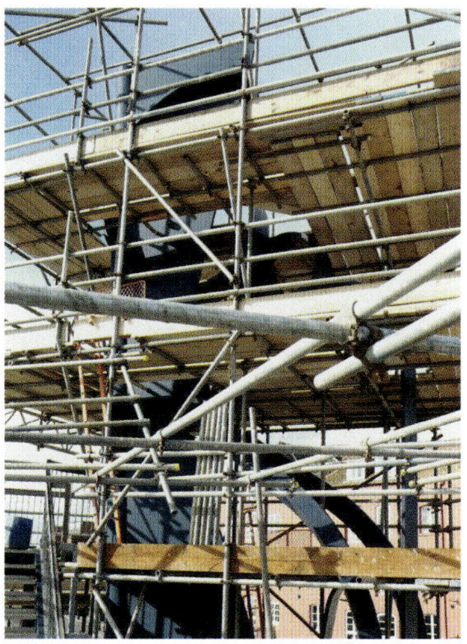

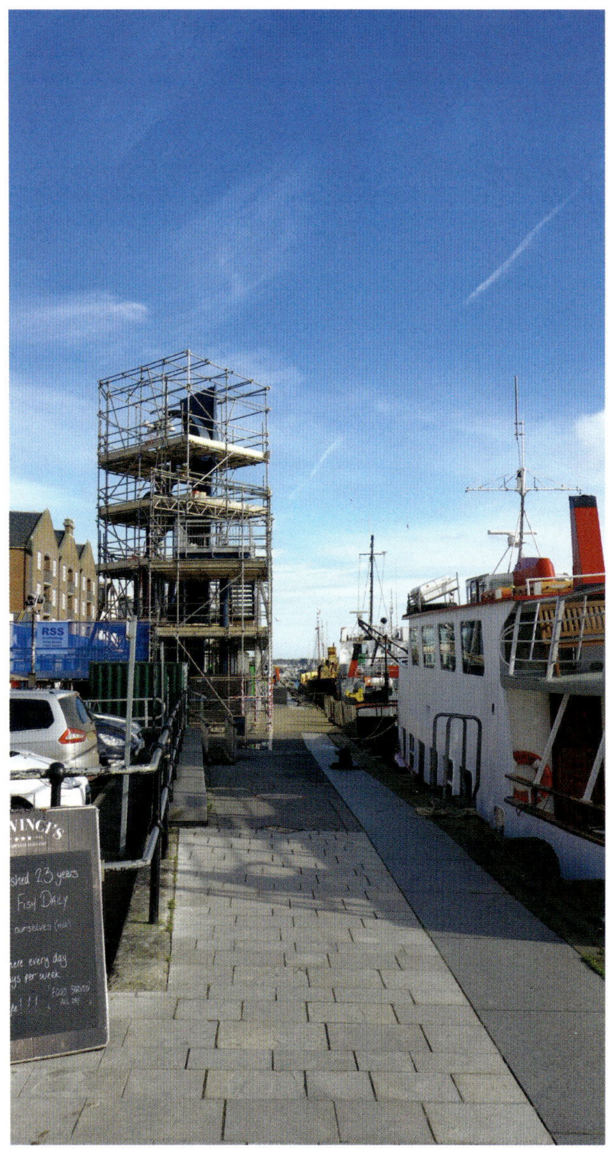
RSS

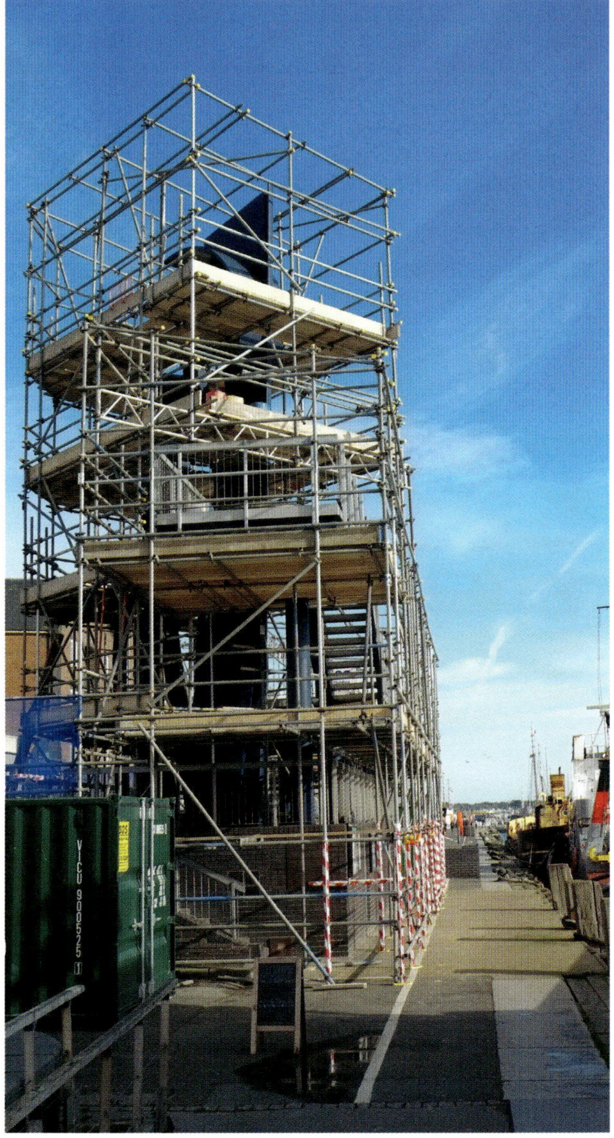

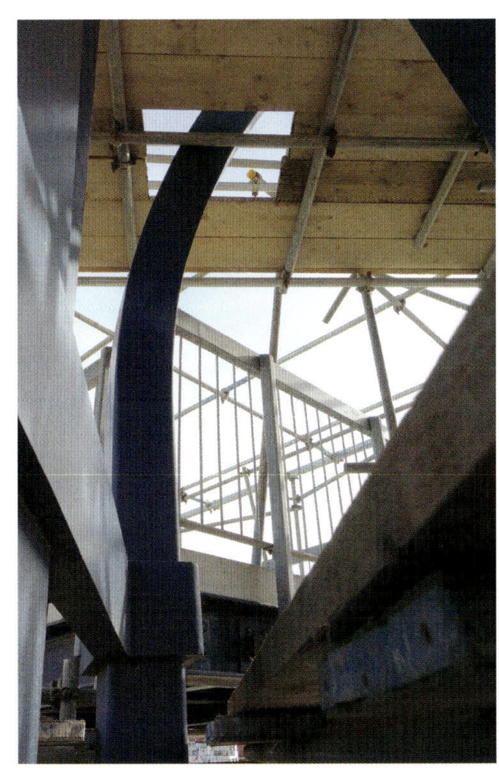
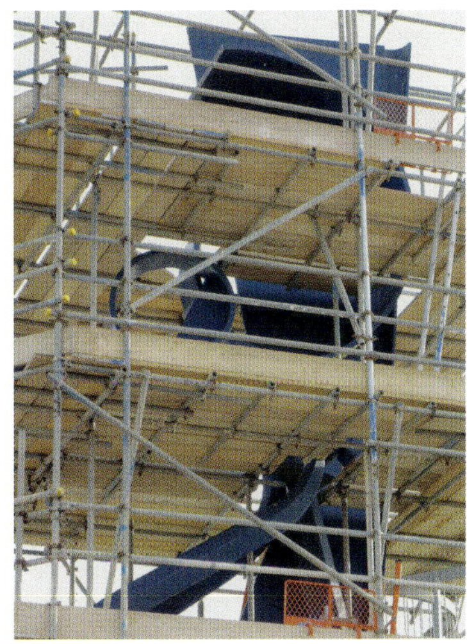
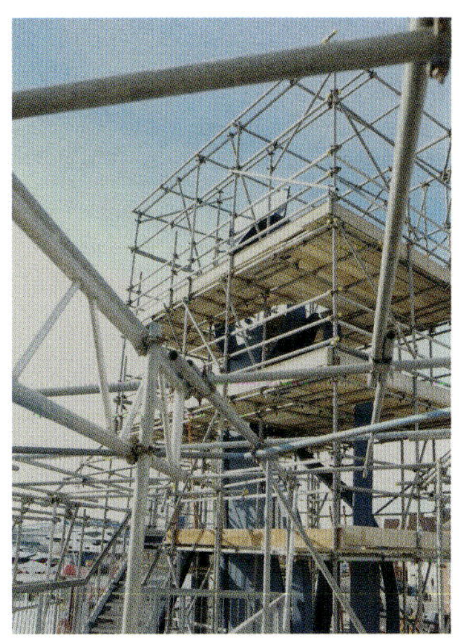
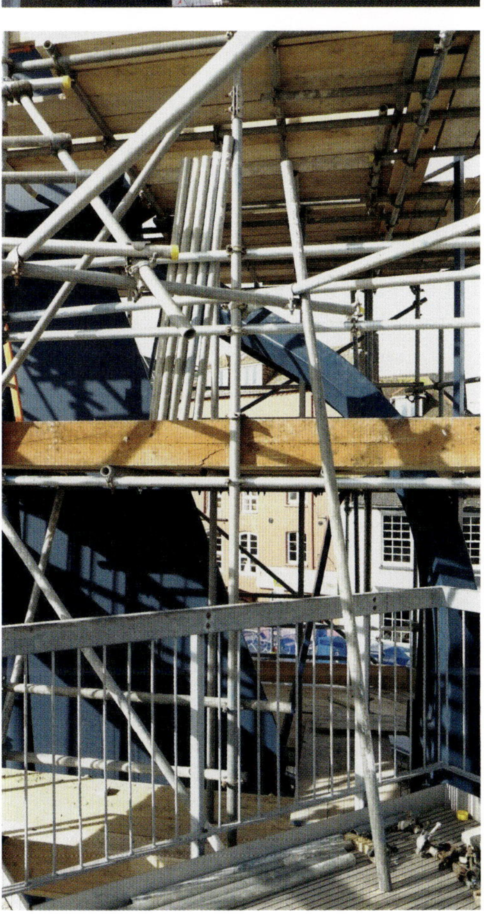
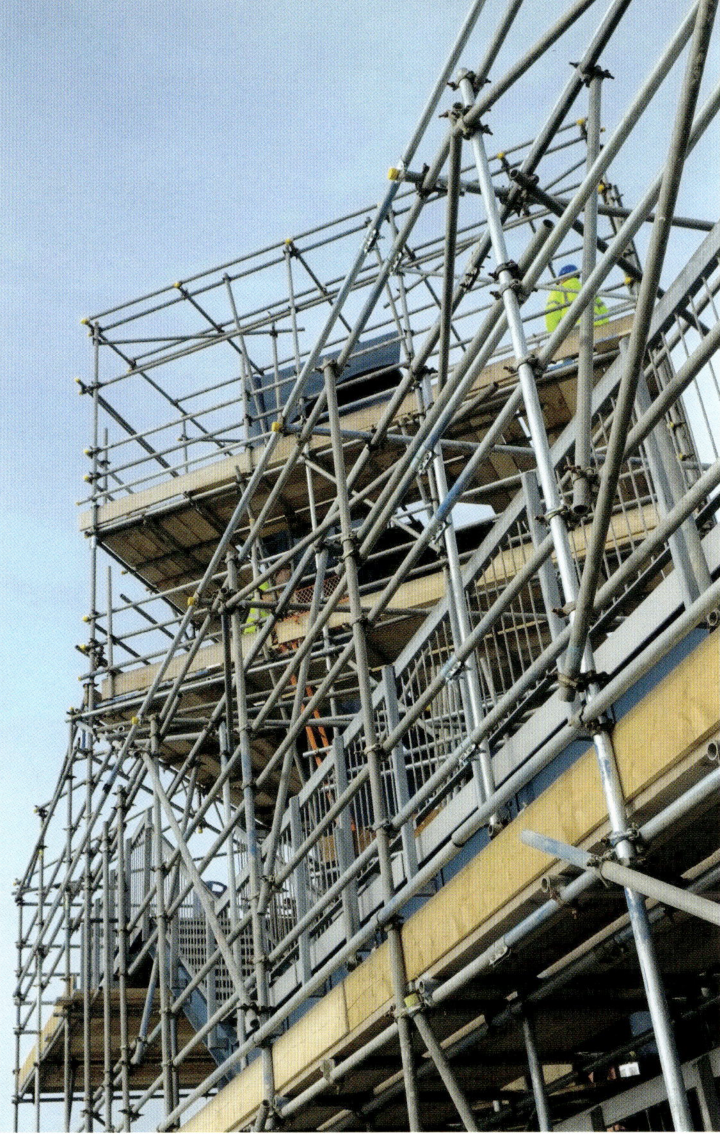

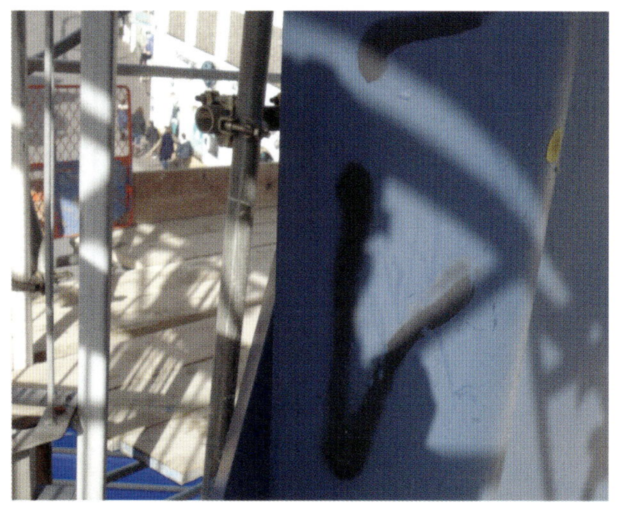

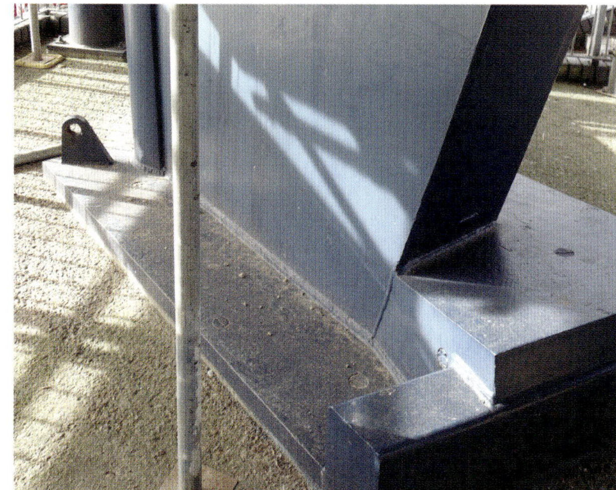

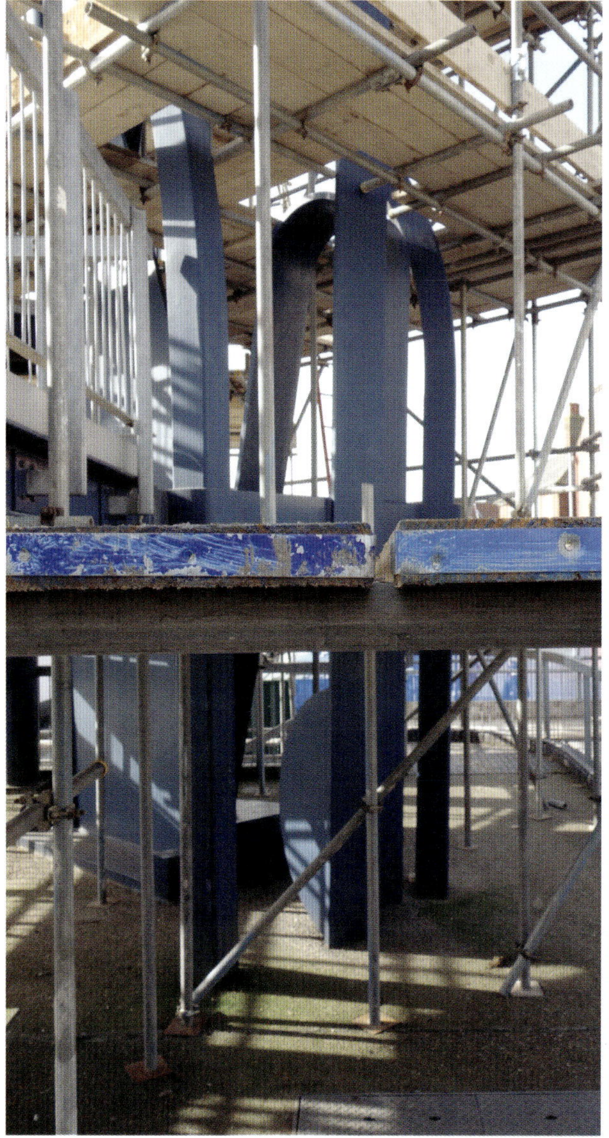

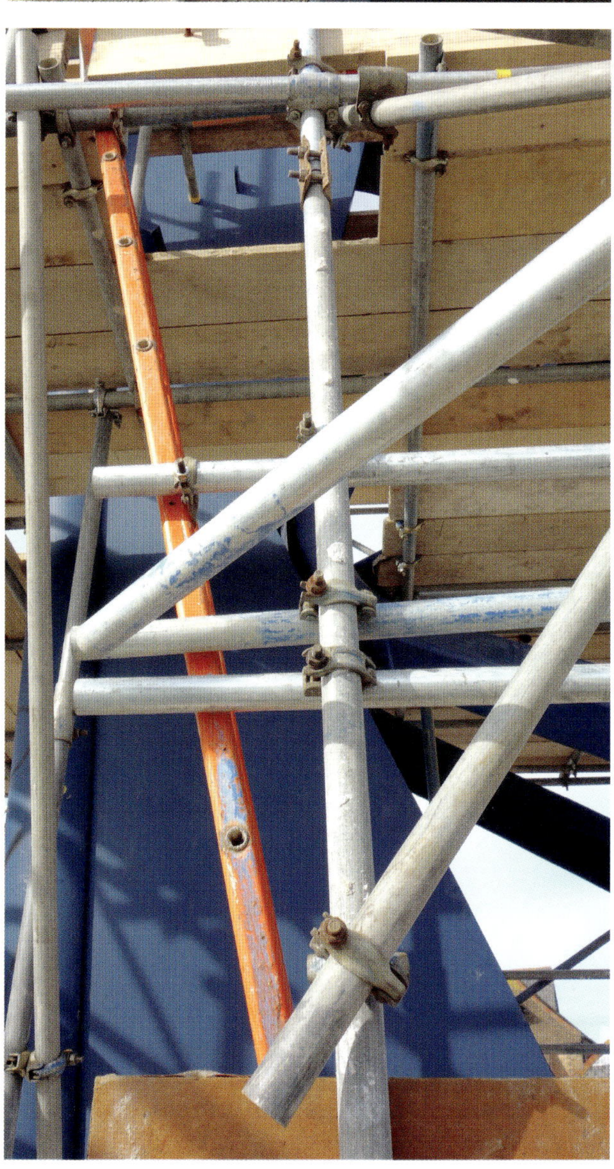

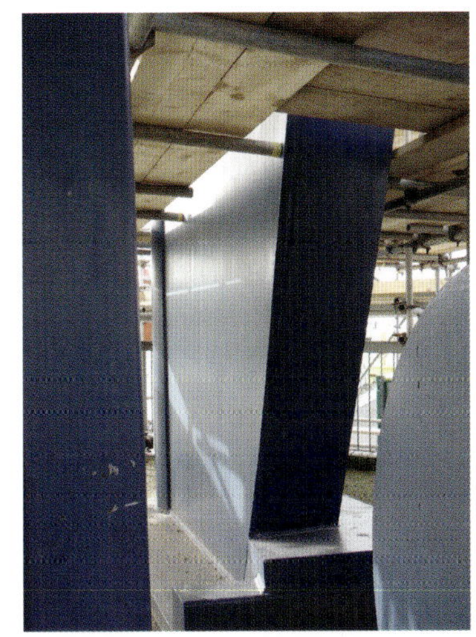

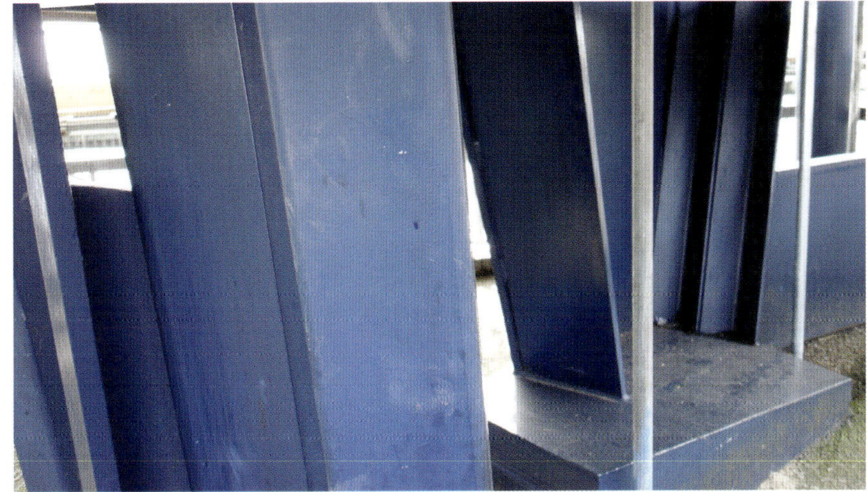

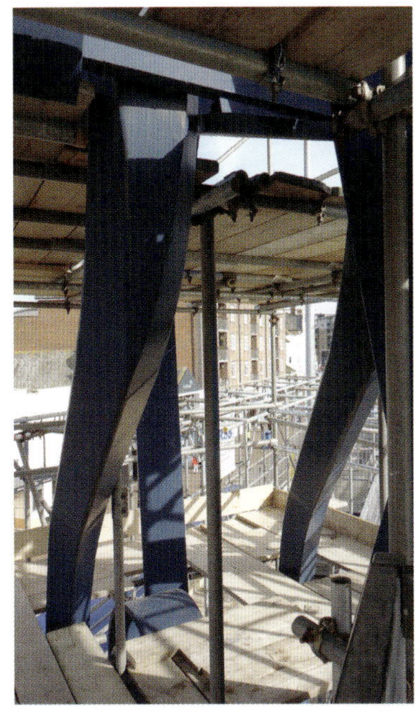

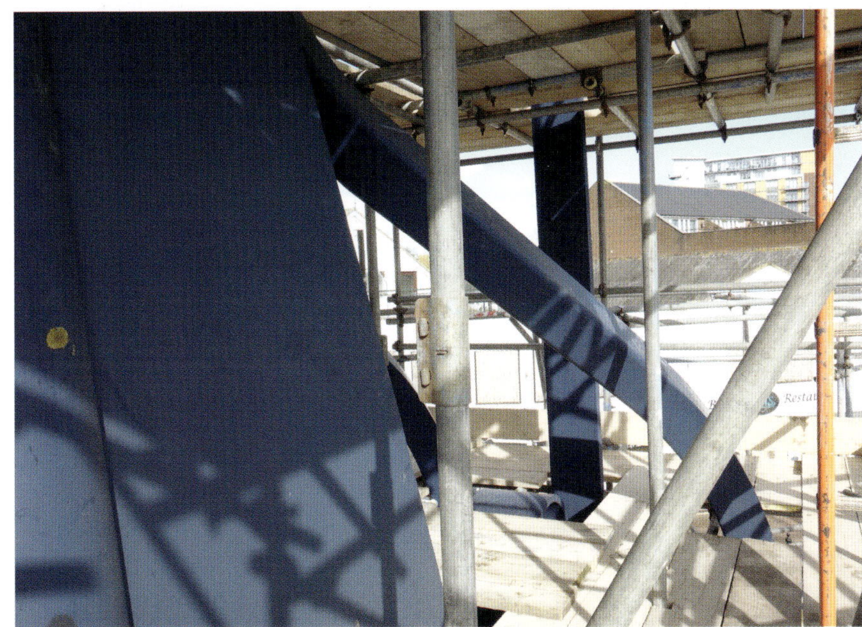

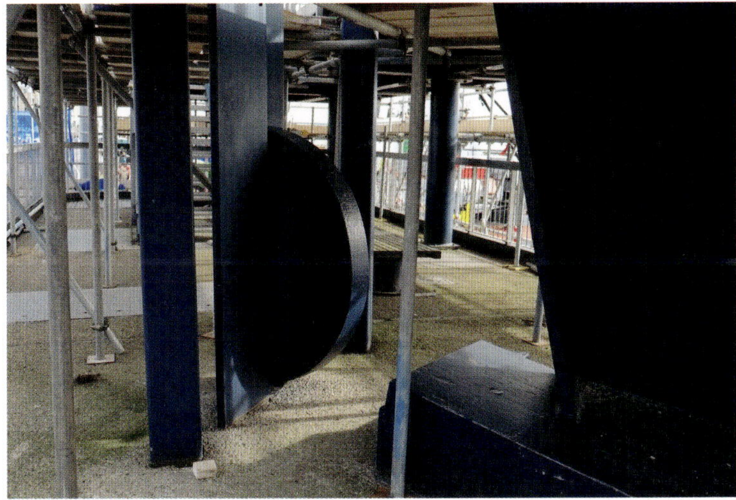

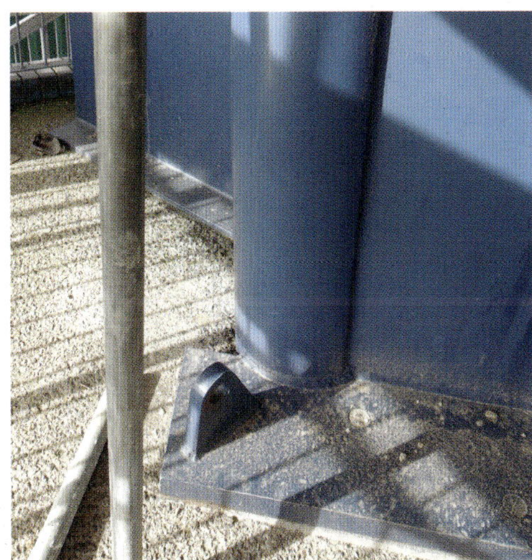

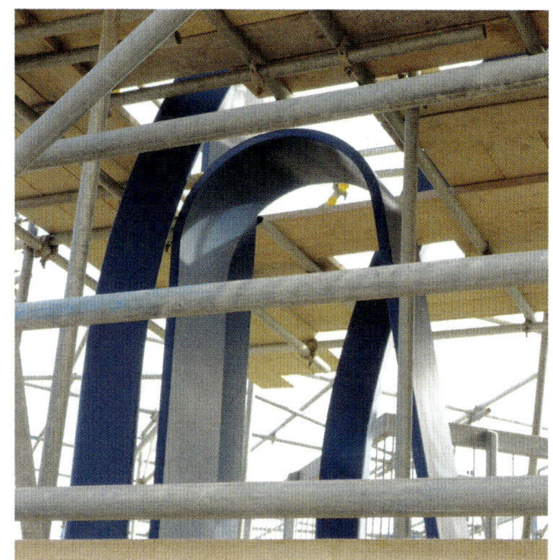
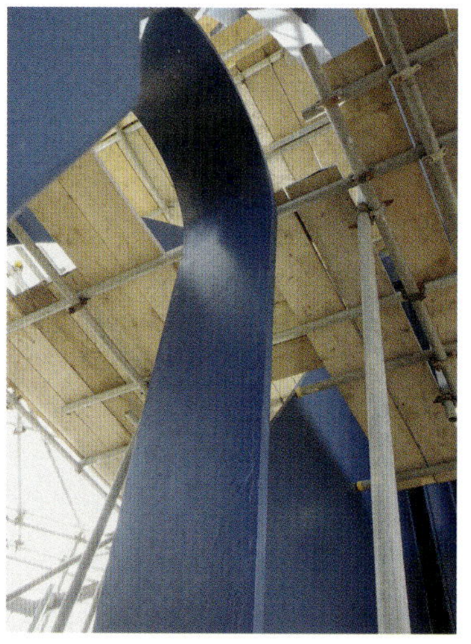
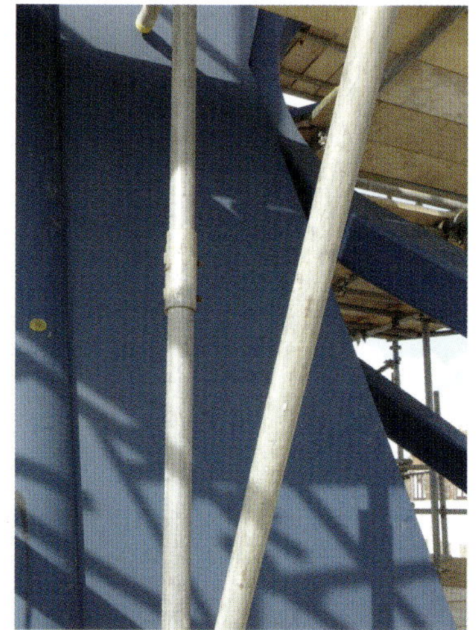
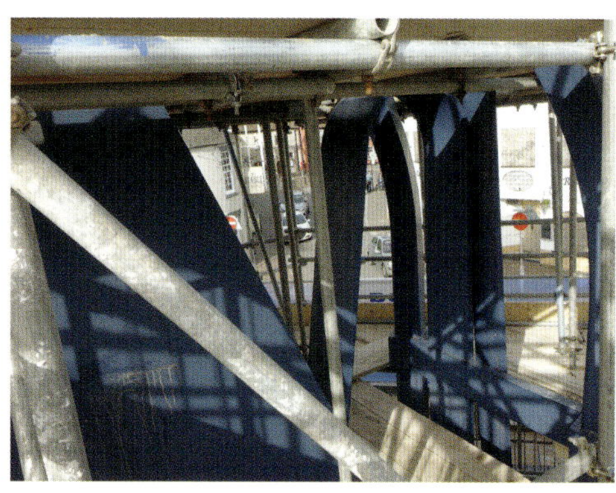
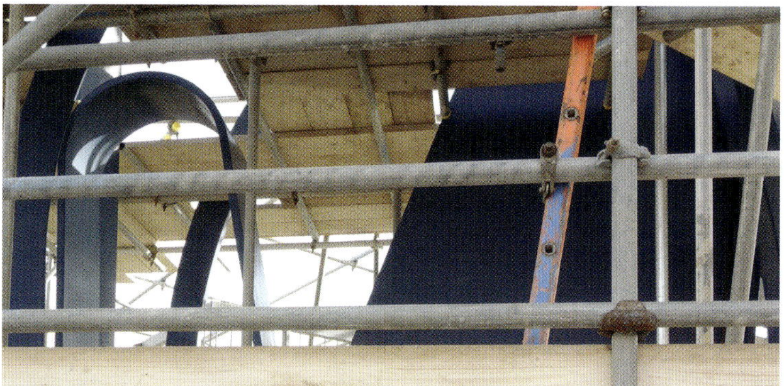
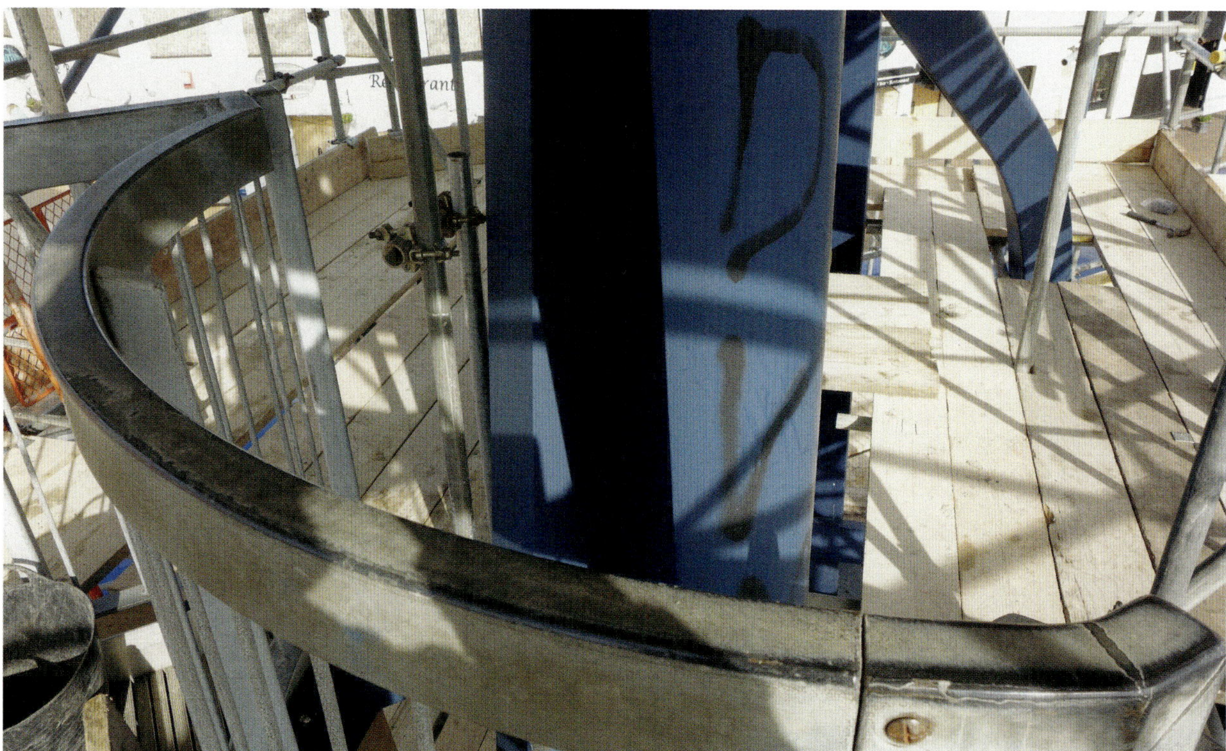

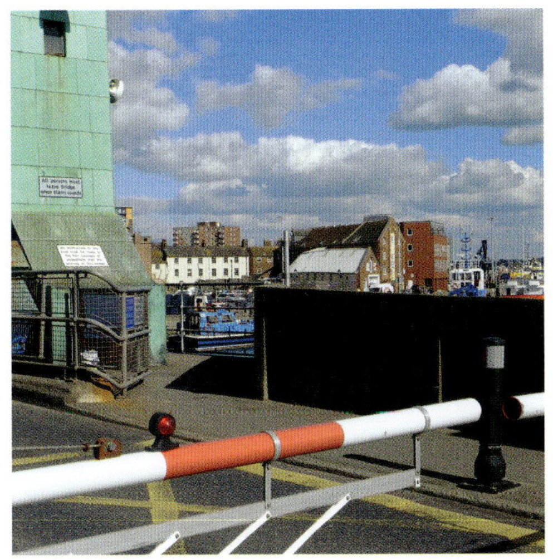
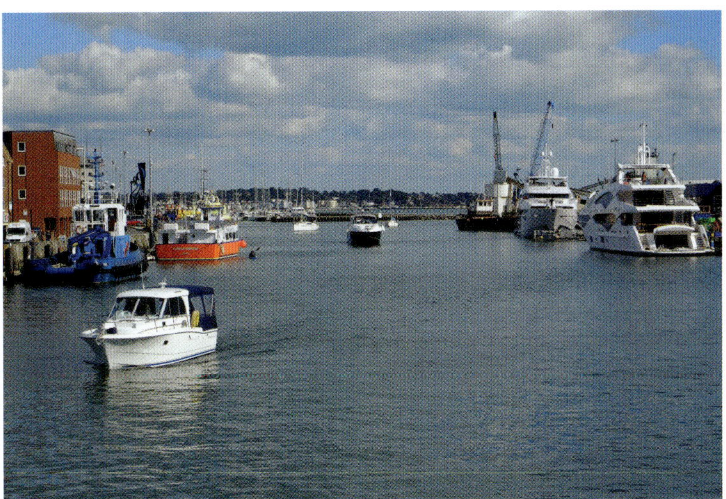
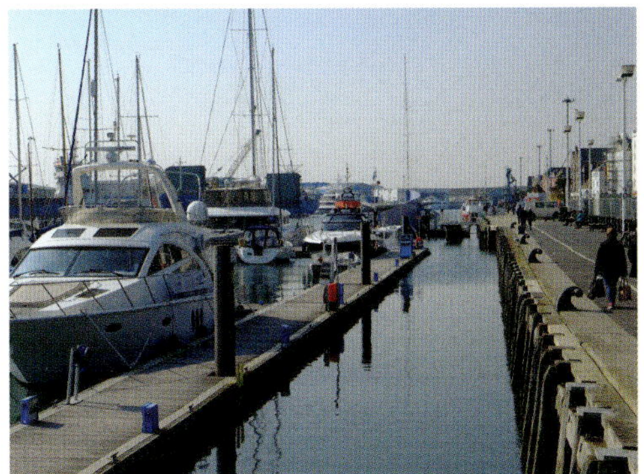
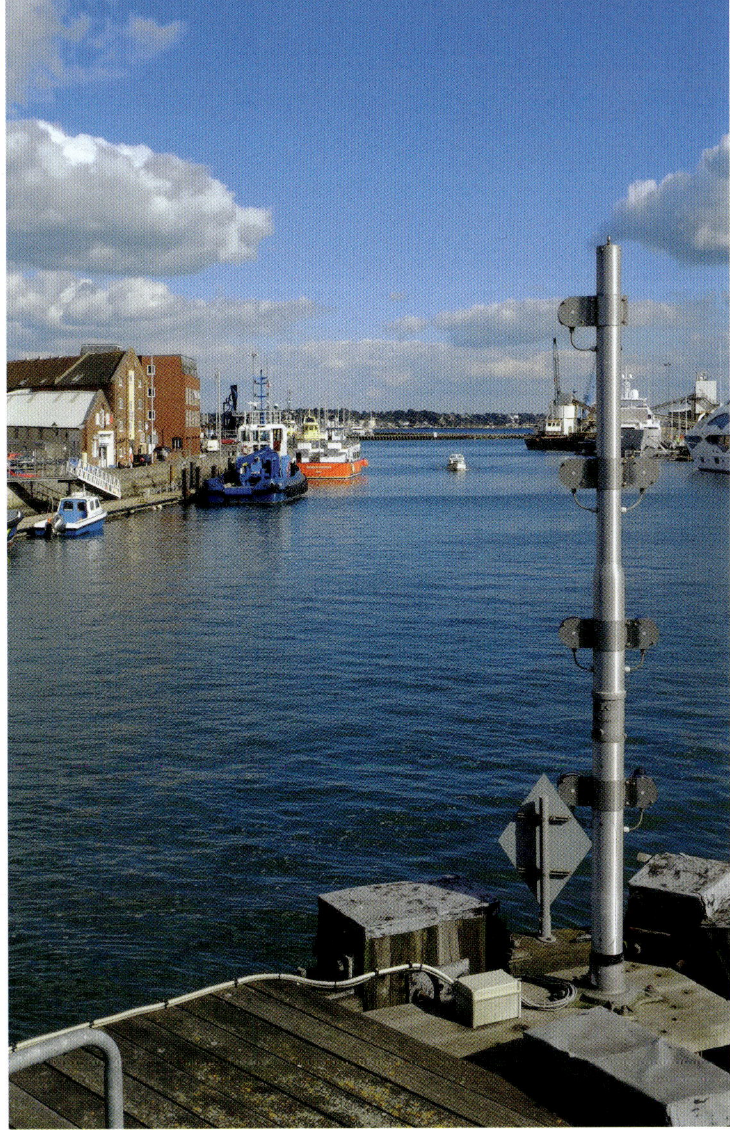
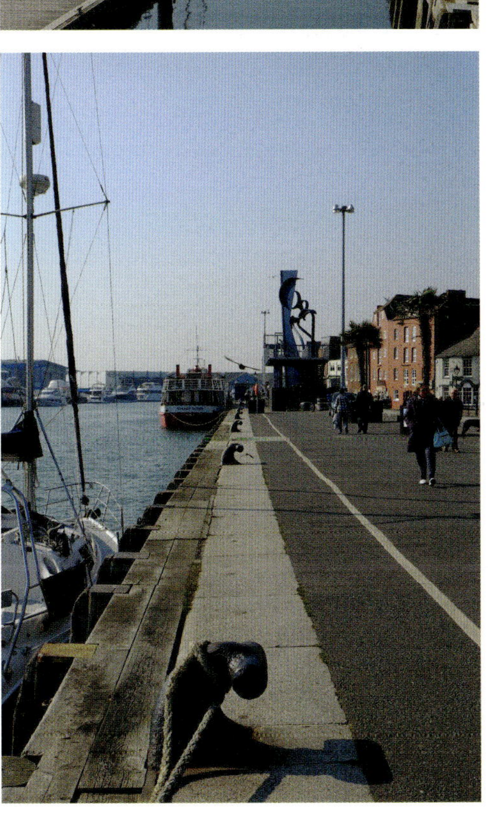

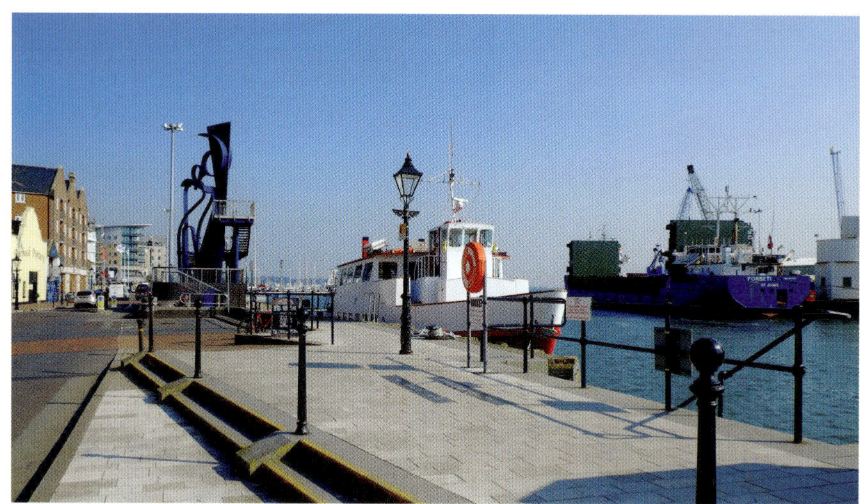
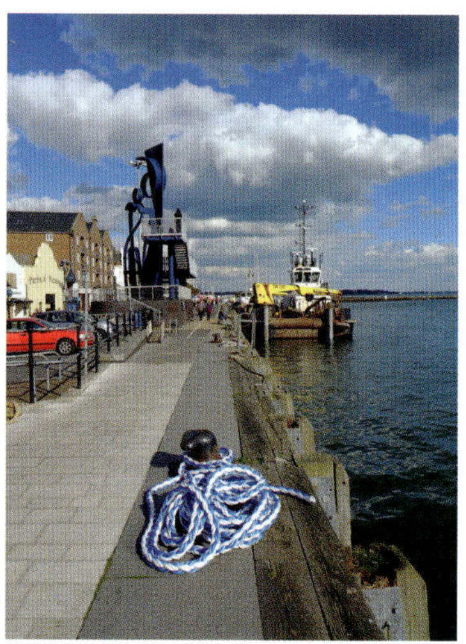
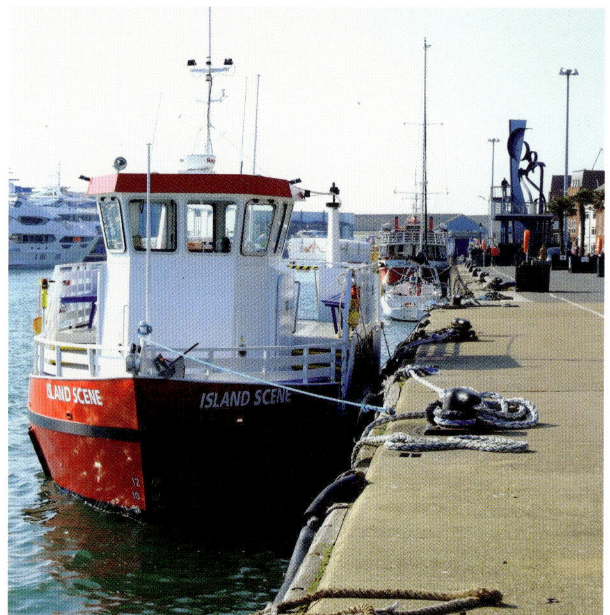
ISLAND SCENE
ISLAND SCENE
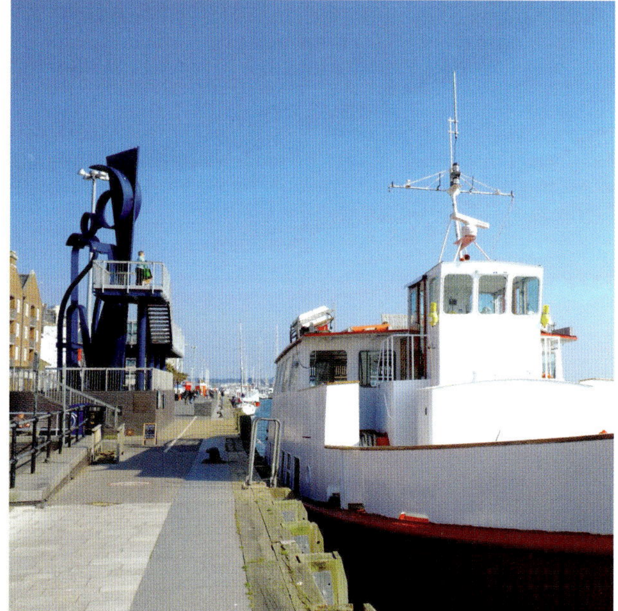
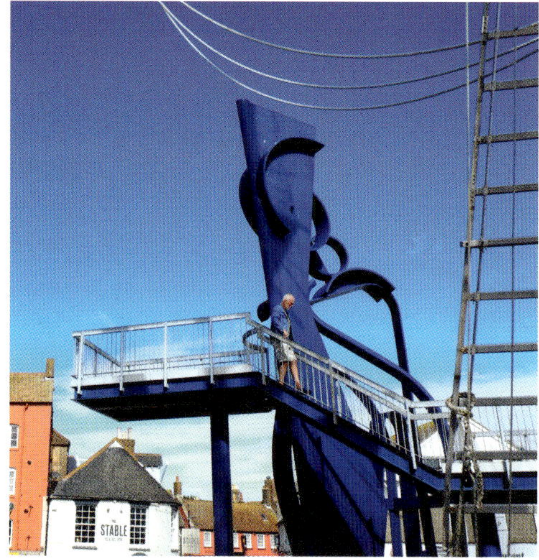
STABLE
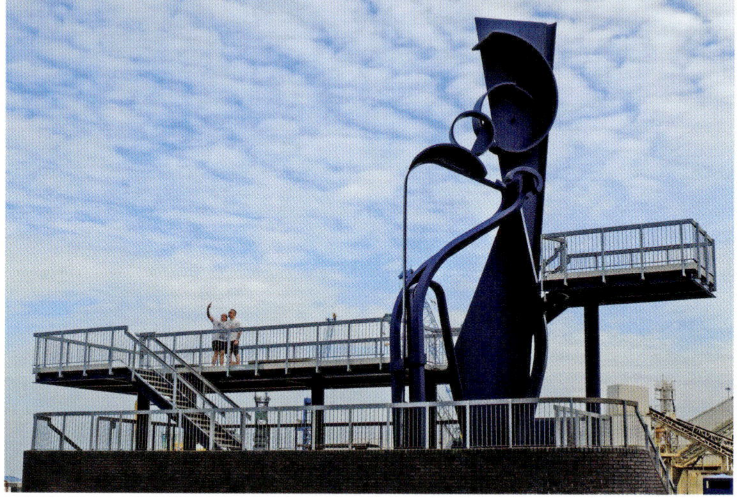

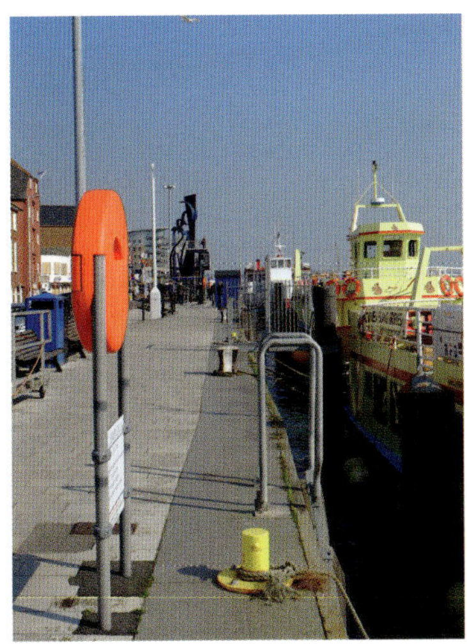

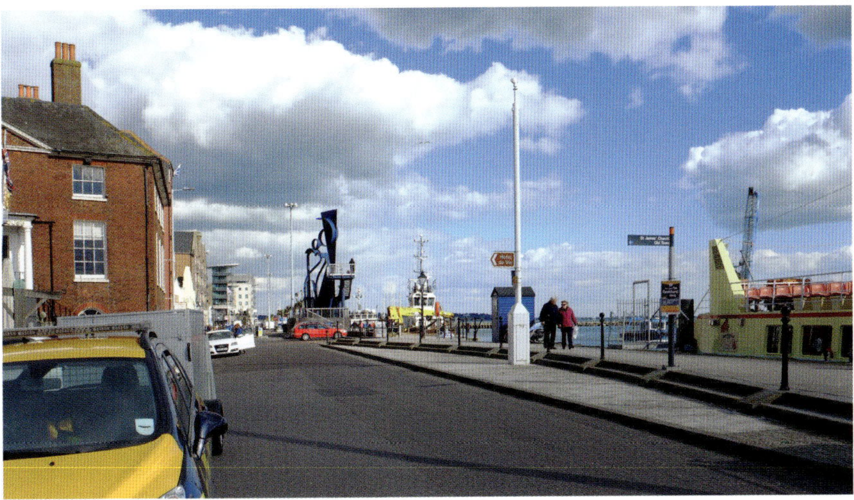

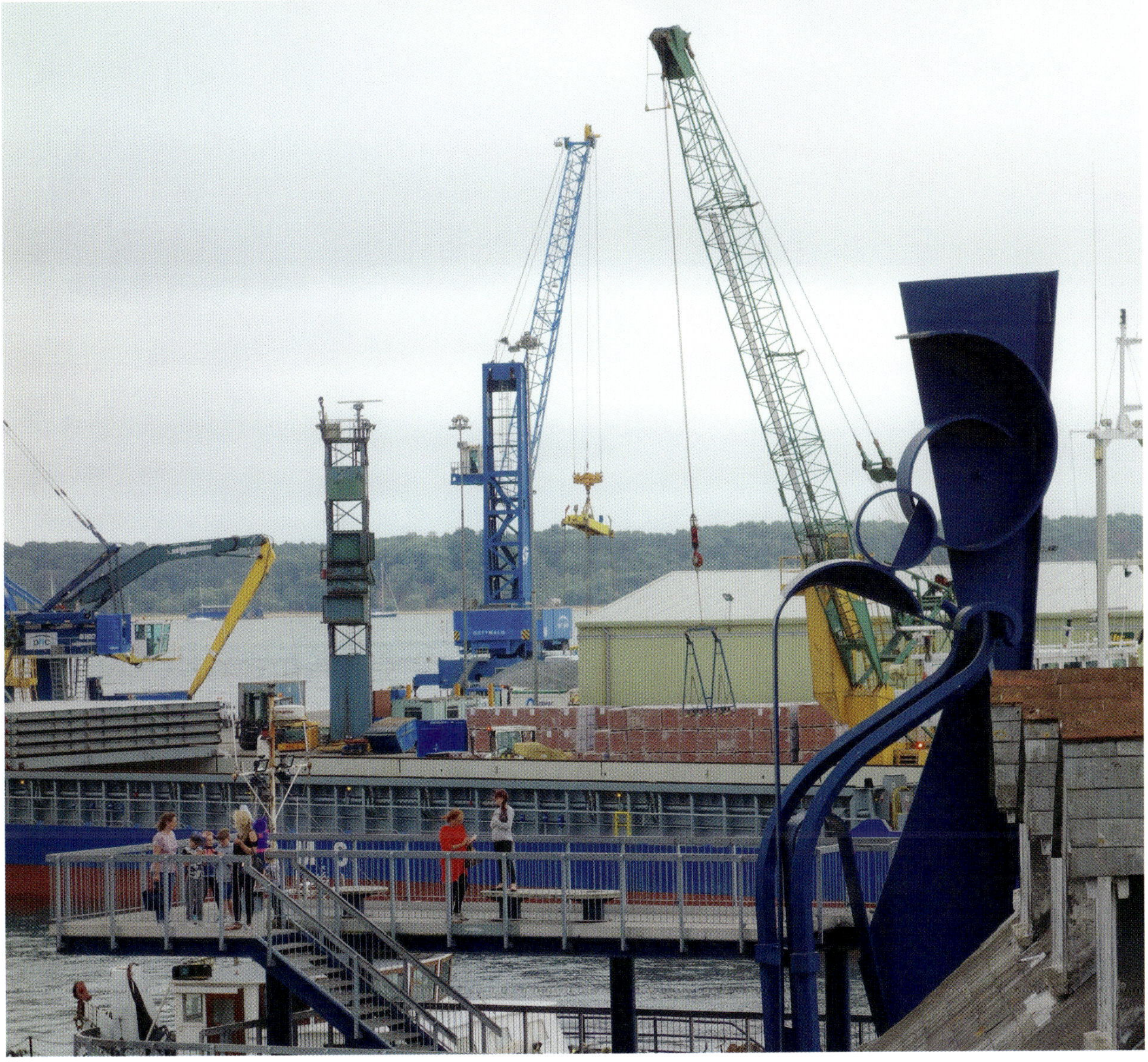

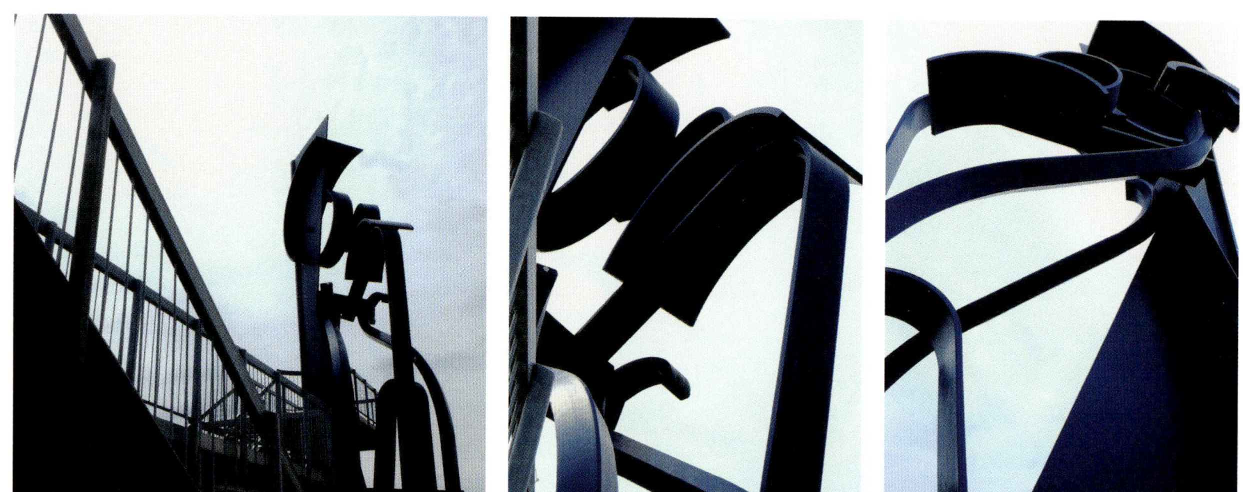

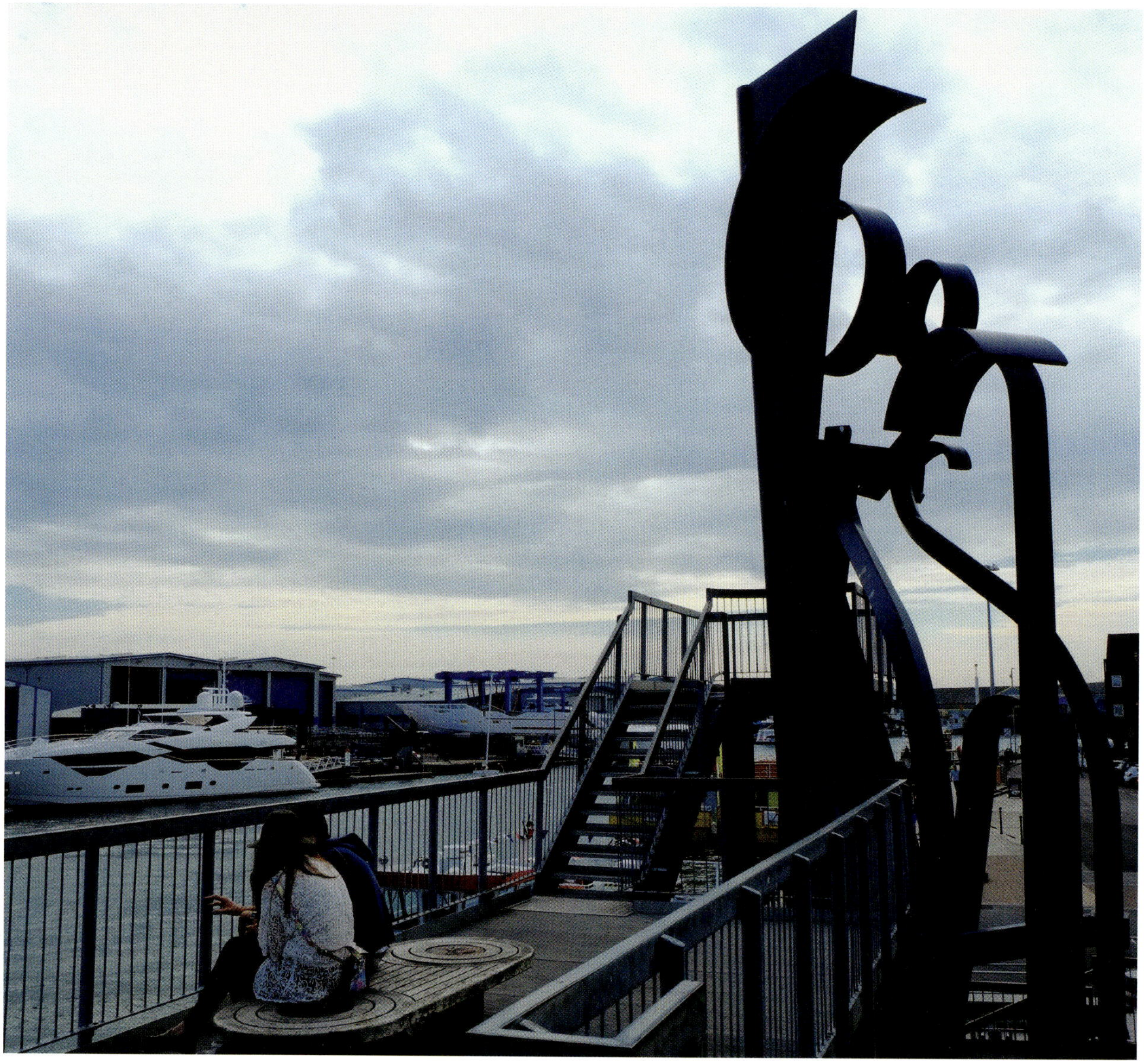

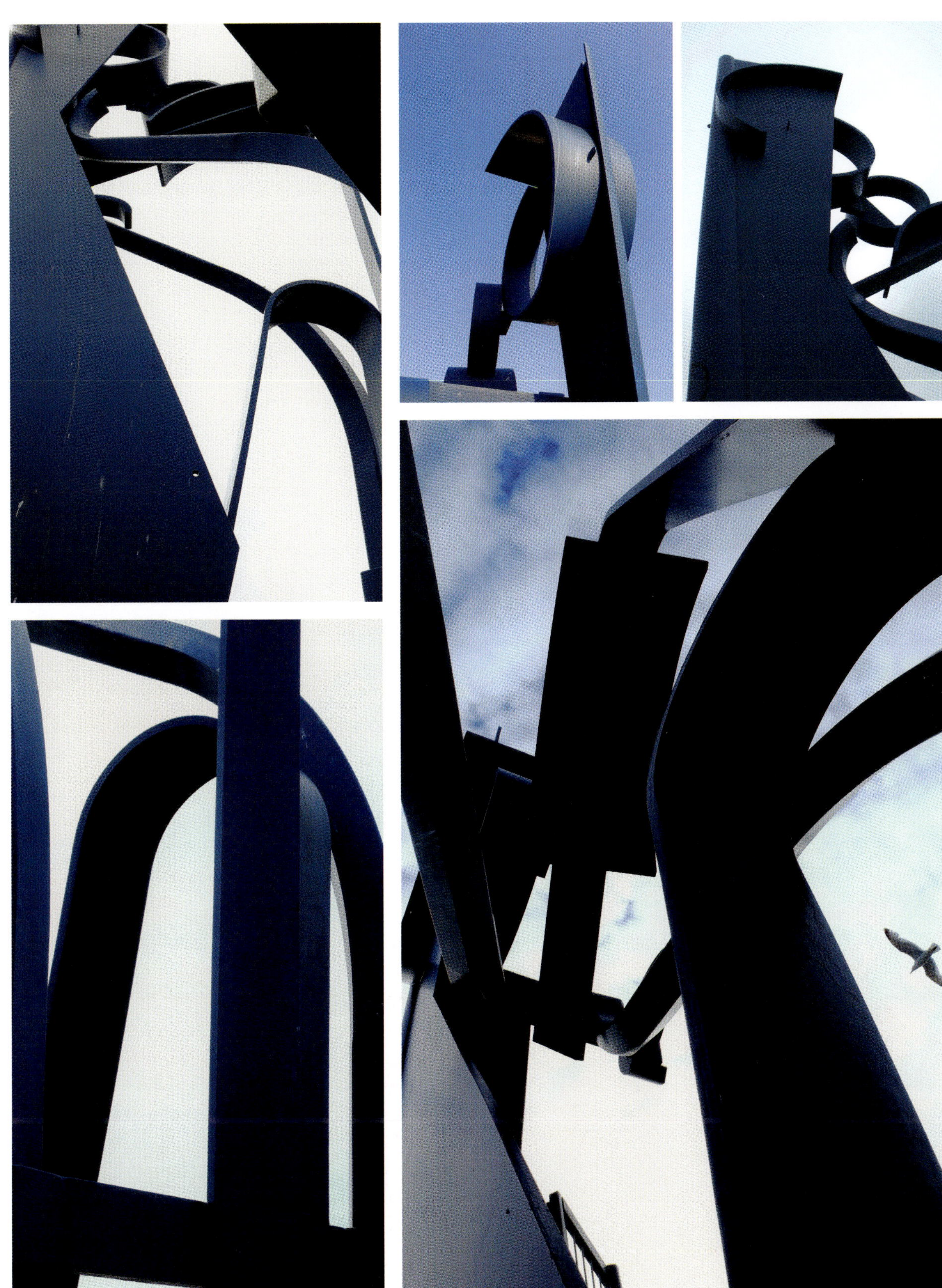

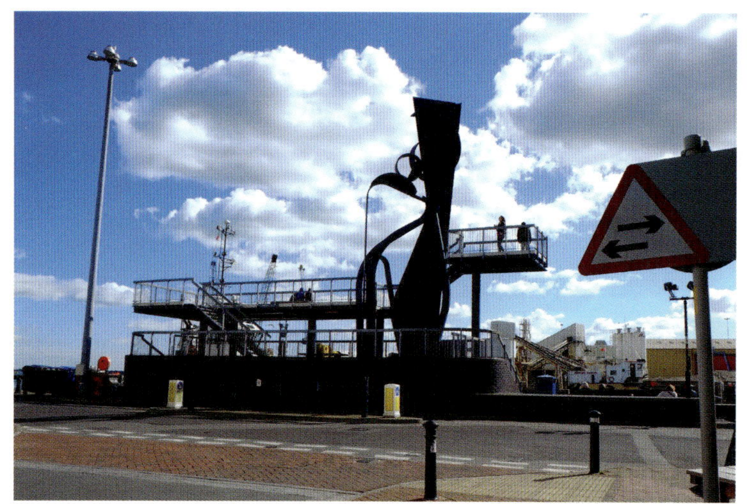

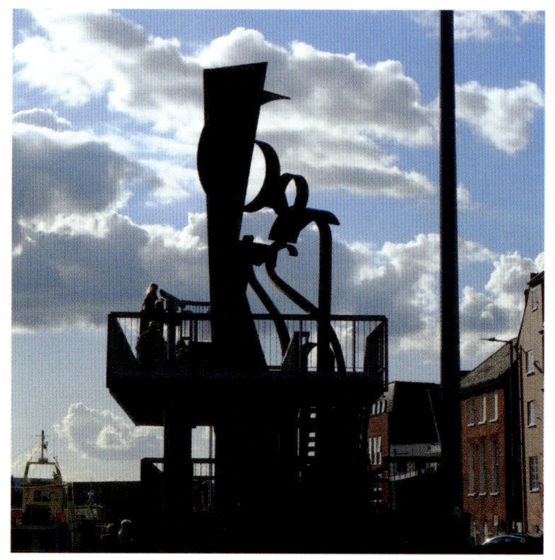

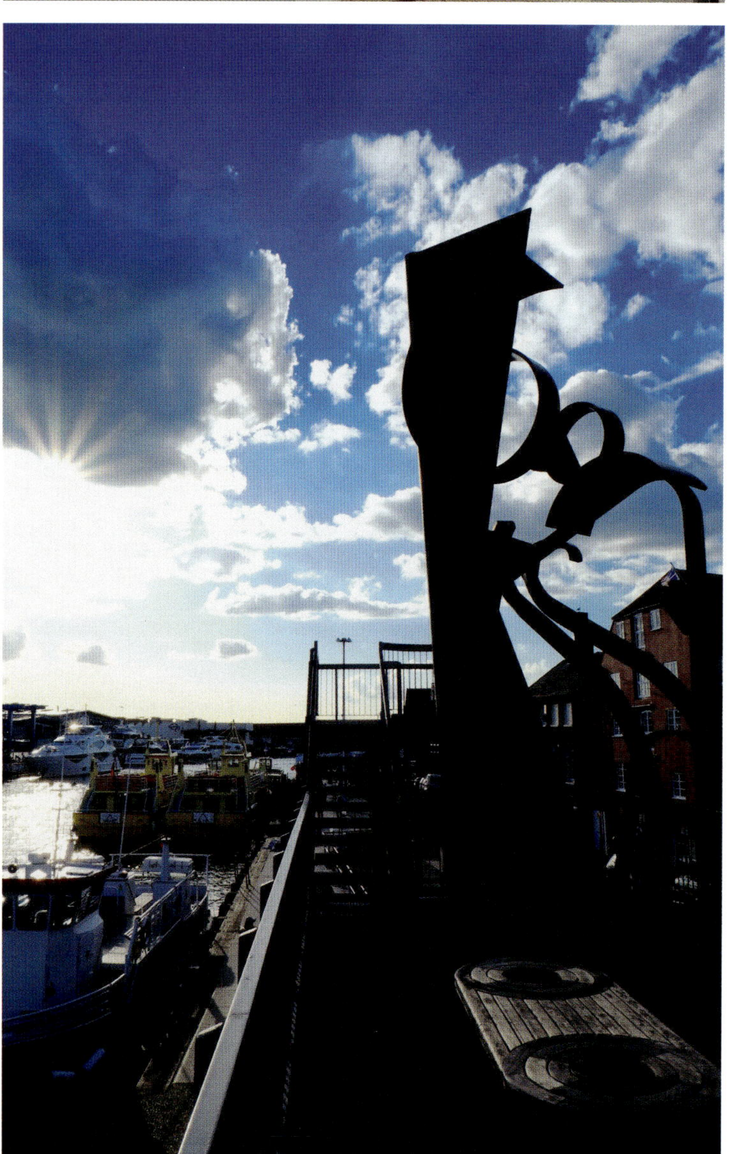

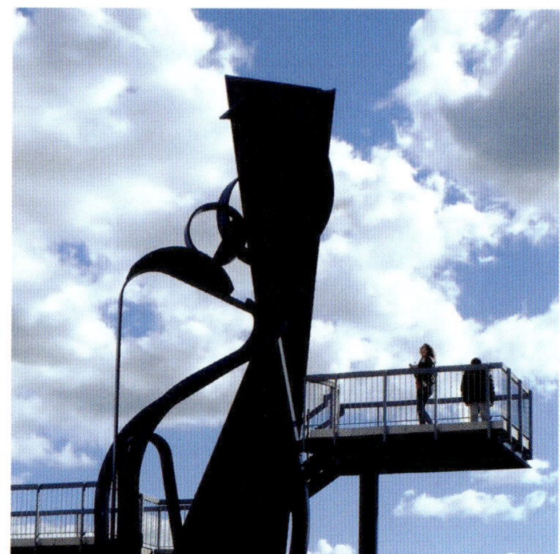

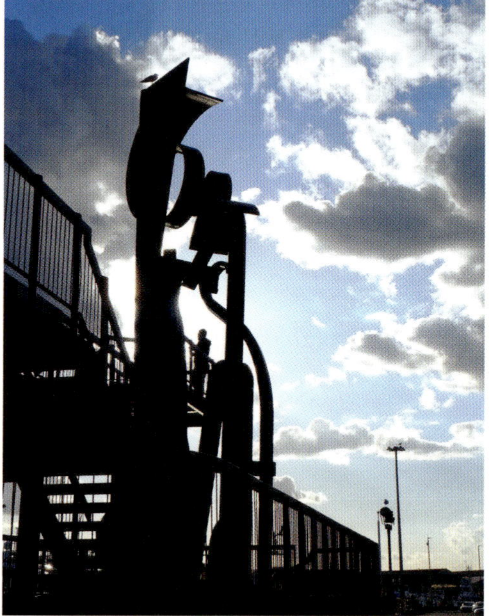

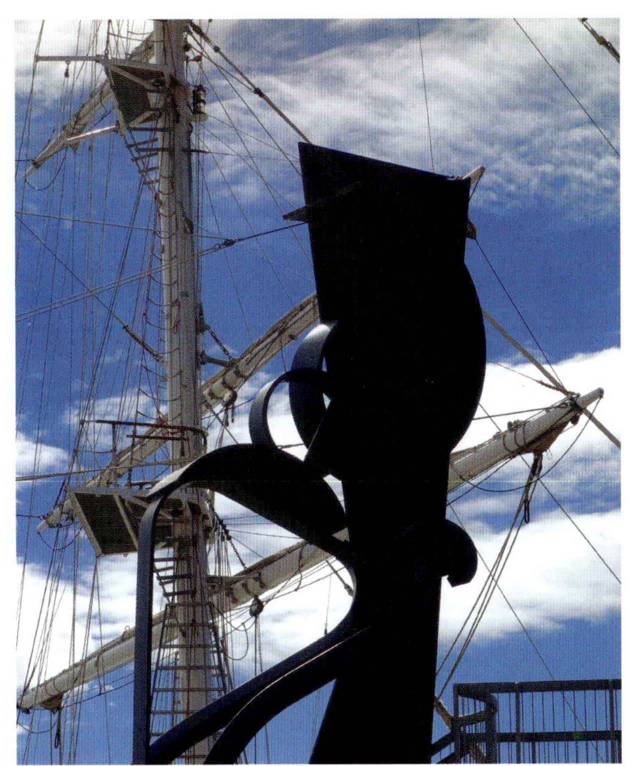

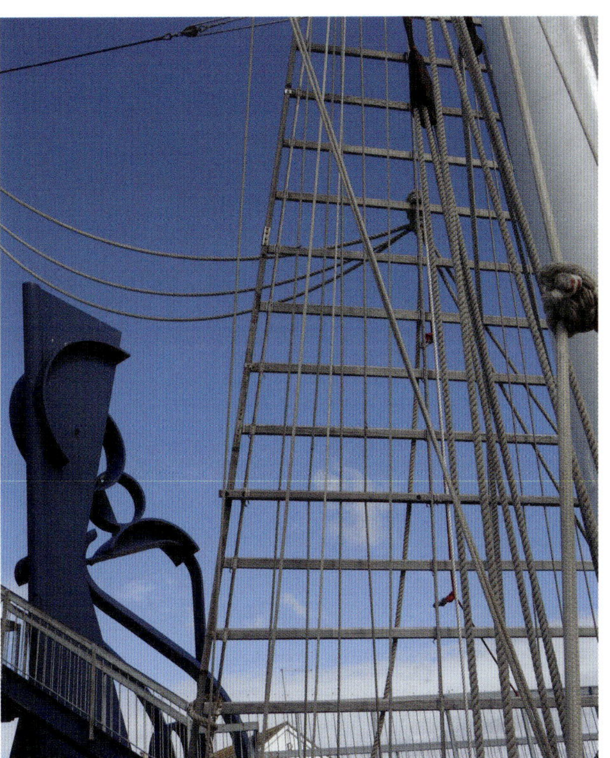

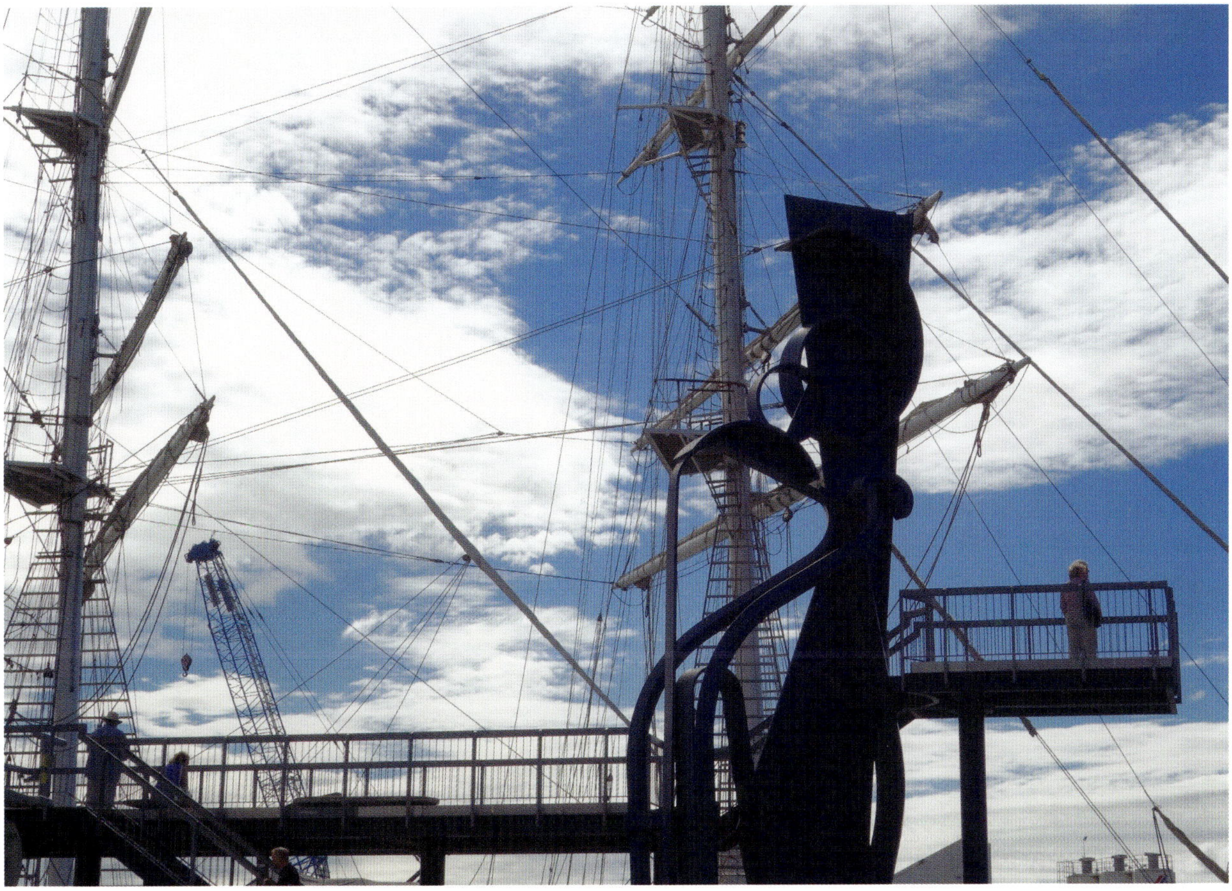

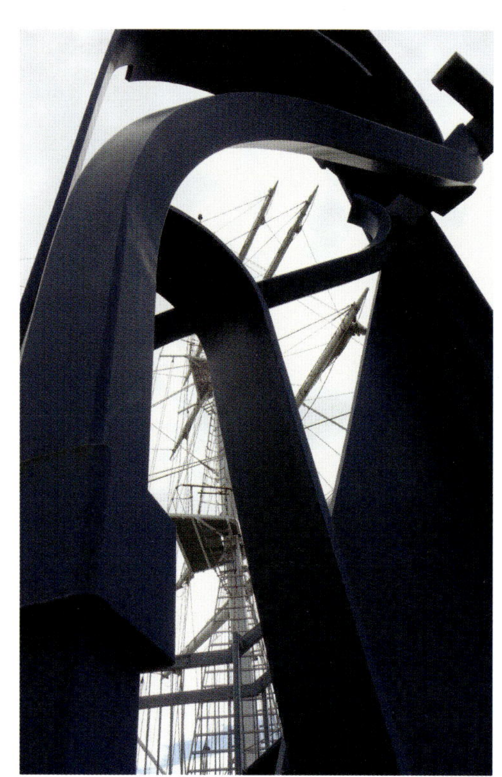
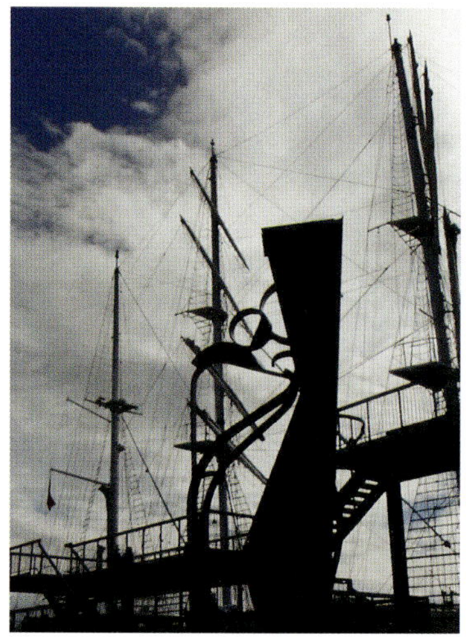
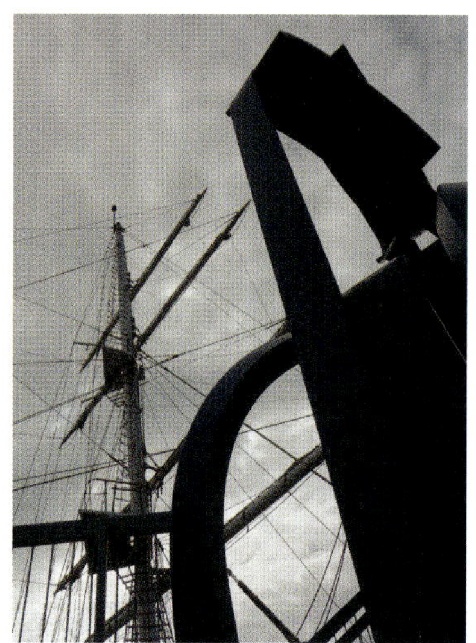
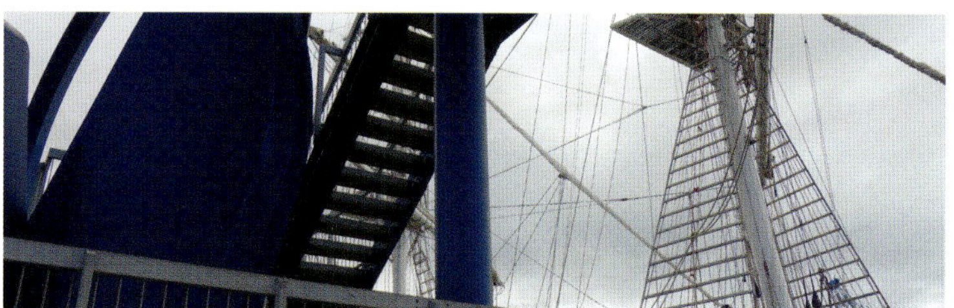

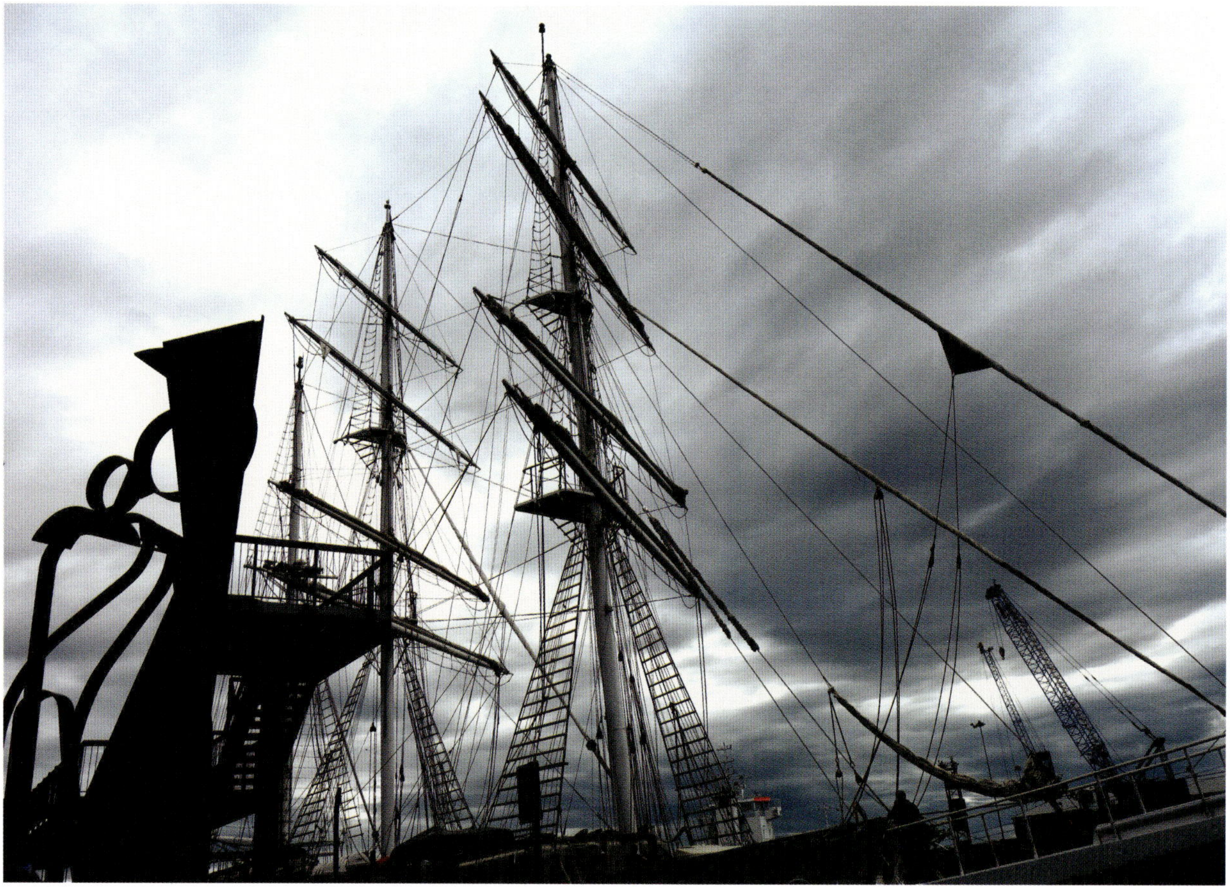

Sculpture into Song

Canford Heath Junior School

The sea surrounds us here in Poole,
The hairy captain sails pirate ships so tall.
He sees birds, fish and islands afar,
With Sea Music in the distance, how lucky we are.

CHORUS:
Sea Music on Poole Quay
Sea Music by Anthony
Sea Music made of steel
Sea Music welded 'til real

Looking out on the shining sea,
Sparkly waves splash the harbour so peacefully.
Sea Music stands straight and tall,
While seafarers are hungry for fish and more.

CHORUS

The seafarer captain out at sea,
Catching sparkly fish so easily,
While Caro was thinking of welding and sparks,
Was the sculpture cold, hot, metal or hard?

CHORUS

Sea Music so blue like the sky and sea,
It looks sharp, scary and very wiggly,
The structure so strong with curvy lines,
Caro leaves art from olden days, behind.

CHORUS

Sea Music in Context

Stephen Feeke

As a triumphant celebration of the twenty-fifth anniversary of *Sea Music*, 120 pupils from Canford Heath Junior School assembled on the sculpture to perform the song they had written. Having taken part in a series of workshops inspired by Anthony Caro's sculpture, their initial responses were developed into lyrics and music with the help of a professional musician.[1] For the assembled audience, the children's enthusiasm for *Sea Music* was refreshing and inspiring. Reading the lyrics opposite their simplicity belies the depth of knowledge and understanding the children acquired about Caro and his processes, and the sense of pride they feel for such a significant work of sculpture located in their home town. The experience of this group of seven- to eight-year-olds is a great lesson to us all. The sculptural language Caro developed can seem complex. His work is not always easy to understand but it does reward the time and effort taken to appreciate it.

Sir Anthony Caro OM CBE RA had a long and prestigious career. He is renowned for revolutionising British sculpture in terms of subject, appearance, materials, methods and ideas, breaking away from the European traditions by showing that sculpture could be abstract and need not be dependent on the human figure. Famously, he also dispensed with the plinth. Over a period of some six decades, he became one of Britain's best-known, prolific and decorated artists and one is now able to see his work in just about every major collection around the world as well as here on Poole Quay. He also exhibited his work in an astonishing array of sites: from white cube gallery spaces to Roman ruins and derelict churches, modern city squares and rooftop gardens. His work has also been seen in a number of sculpture parks, in Britain and abroad, including the one which I help to run at Roche Court

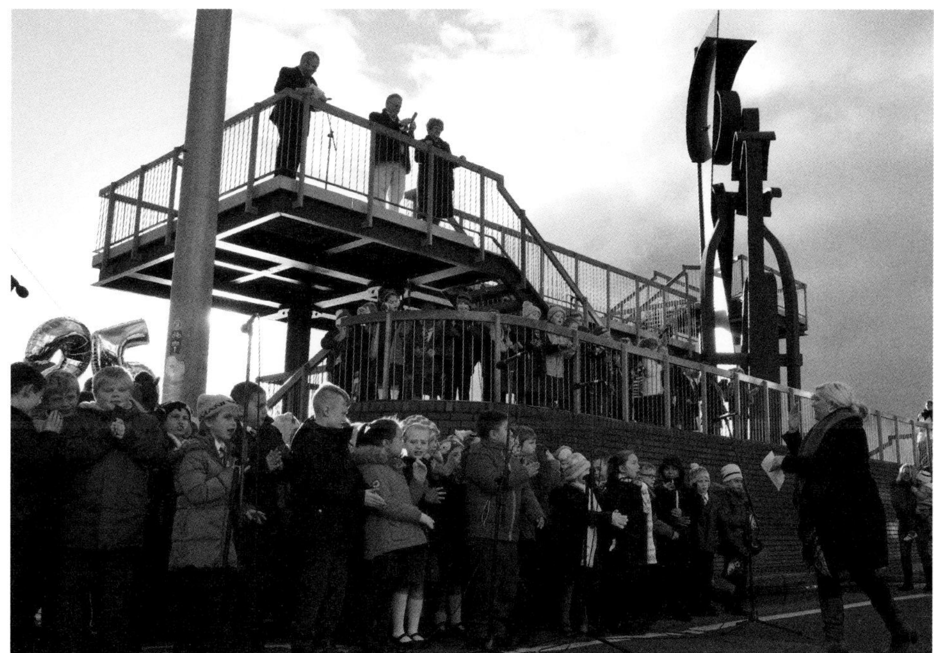

Canford Heath Junior School performing *Sculpture into Song*, 22 November 2016.

and at Chatsworth, for an exhibition that I helped curate. Within an impressive oeuvre, Caro's *Sea Music* is unique; it is the only site-specific, monumental sculpture he ever made for the public realm. Moreover, it is sited on a plinth of sorts, a water pumping station situated on Poole Quay. Despite its great size and its rarity, *Sea Music* has been allowed to slip from the greater consciousness; even many of the experts who know Caro's work well are largely unaware of its existence. Newly conserved and saved for the future, this is an opportunity to reassess *Sea Music* and to begin celebrating it as an important example of the artist's work and a major public sculpture.

In many ways the fate of *Sea Music* over the past twenty-five years illustrates how problematic a public sculpture can be. Whilst it figures largely in all the events held on Poole Quay, a work can sometimes become so familiar, it becomes a part of the site, almost invisible and ignored. Conversely, works that result from public-spirited commissions can easily become targets of negative criticism. They can attract graffiti, or worse, they become an object of theft, valued more as scrap than as art. If sculpture outside is vulnerable in many more ways than sculpture inside, it is also much harder to site. Within the confines of a gallery, the curator uses architecture as a kind of framework when placing a sculpture. The extant lines of walls and doorways in a building offer a formal structure with which to align the work, which can give a sense of power to the placement and can concentrate our attention. A site outdoors is inevitably more fluid, and the flux of the environment cannot be controlled. Variations in nature continuously alter the context, as changing seasons and weather conditions transform the outdoor space. There are also more distractions

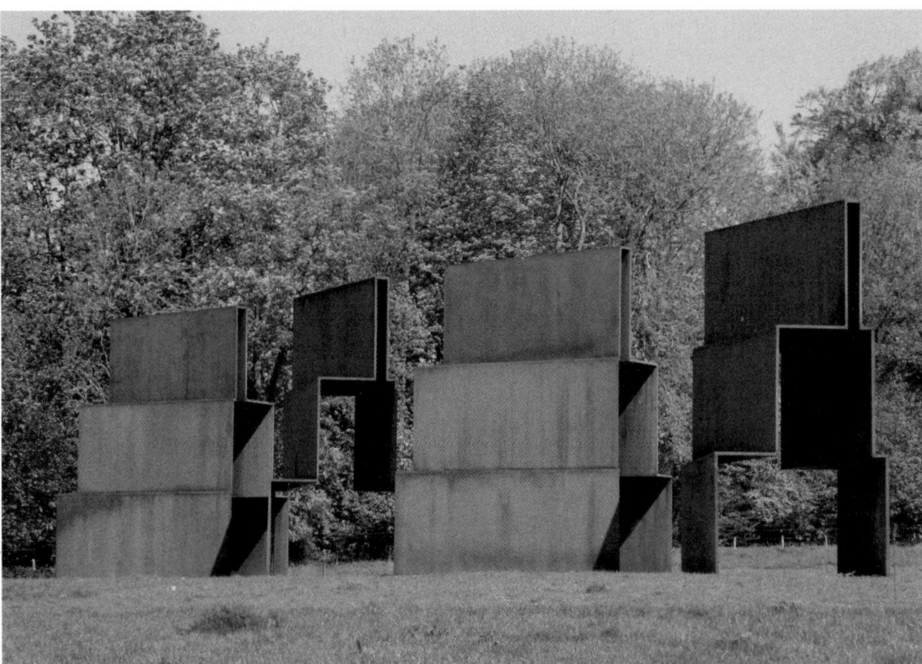

Anthony Caro, *Millbank Steps* (2004) in the sculpture park at the New Art Centre, Roche Court.

outside to divert the viewer's attention. Yet a well-placed sculpture can give pause, populating a view with an empathetic presence, and the setting allows distance, to see the entirety of a large work from afar. The contiguous walkways of *Sea Music* offer new perspectives and also allow the visitor to experience *Sea Music* more intimately. Up close, the sculpture dominates again and one appreciates fully its size. One is able to study and appreciate its complexity and special lyrical qualities, which lie in the contrast that emerges as the viewer walks up the steps and moves around it, between its many wide, curved surfaces and its dramatic verticals. These different aspects are captured beautifully in David Ward's new series of photographs, which form the plates in this publication. Entitled *One Hundred Views of Sea Music* (2016–17) with a nod to Hokusai's prints of Mount Fuji, they are an artist's depiction of the sculpture as it has been conserved, taken at various times of day, from different locations and viewpoints within Poole, and in various seasons and weather conditions.

Sea Music should also command our attention as it is by an artist who is not routinely associated with the outdoors. Indeed, Caro's preference for interior spaces has often been quoted. Asked early in his career in 1972, by Phyllis Tuchman, whether he evaluated his sculptures by 'considering their appearance inside and outside', Caro responded: 'I prefer my sculpture to be seen in a tranquil and enclosed space. Almost all sculpture, I guess, needs to be indoors – or enclosed in some way; it mostly blows away if it's in the open air, or else it becomes environment' – and further claimed that 'all my sculpture (however large) is unpublic'.[2] But given the presence of *Sea Music* and how often Caro did in fact show his work outdoors, his statement is worth recontextualising here.

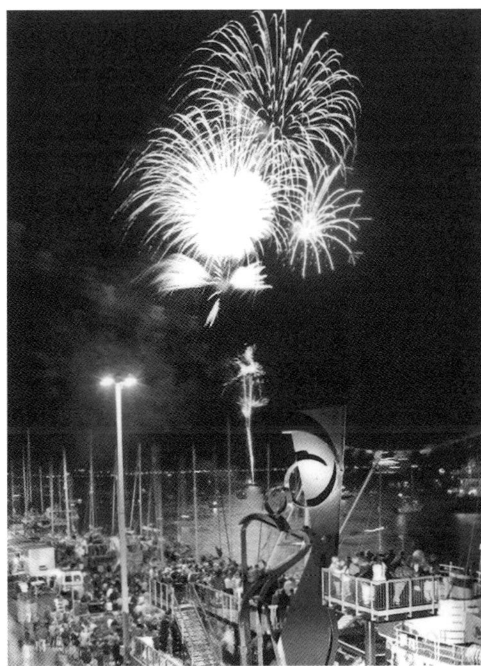

Sea Music on Poole Quay during the summer firework display, c.1998. Photo: Suzanne Sieger

Caro studied engineering before serving in the Royal Navy during the Second World War (experiences which, with the benefit of hindsight, seem particularly relevant to *Sea Music*). He later studied sculpture at the Royal Academy between 1947 and 1952. The focus of his formative artistic training was on techniques and skill. In this rather traditional, insular world there was little discussion about what an art work could be about. Sculpture was ostensibly architectural decoration: fountains in parks or large portraits of important men on horseback in a prominent position on a pedestal. By 1951 he felt he had reached the limit of what the Academy could teach him. He knew Henry Moore was the most important modern sculptor working at the time and, unannounced, went to visit him. Six months later Caro started working for Moore part-time. Caro later acknowledged how crucial this period was in his development as an artist. Moore allowed him to borrow books on painting, sculpture, architecture and African and Oceanic art. His mind became full of images and ideas. Moore and Caro also had many discussions about the possibilities for sculpture and the forms it could take.

In 1953 Caro began teaching at Saint Martin's School of Art and established himself as an independent artist. He met other artists and, crucially, architects such as Richard Rogers. He described his teaching as a form of discovery, finding what sculpture could be in terms of subject, materials and methods. He felt figurative sculpture had been drained of expressive potential and wanted to find new ways for sculpture, to convey meaning and feeling. It wasn't just the materials and processes which were important to him, 'what was important was the whole examination of what sculpture could be to you in your life. It was no longer an object to put on a mantelpiece and forget about, or to be seen from a distance on a hill top. It was a question of how it could be far more immediate.'[3]

By the time of Caro's first important exhibition held at the Whitechapel Art Gallery in 1963, he was credited with throwing open the idea of what sculpture could be. He used visible steel I-beams, circular aluminium tubes and sheets of steel, welded and bolted together. The work was not an enclosed solid form; it had been opened up and extended. It was about the relationships between lightness and weight, balance and gravity, space and volume. Each element had a complex formal relationship to the other parts which unfold as the viewer walks around the work. Linear elements activated the surrounding space, implying a trace of the artist's own movements as he created the sculpture. An important feature was also his use of colour.

Caro continued teaching at Saint Martin's until 1979, but he also taught at Bennington College in Vermont from 1953 to 1965. In the US he saw the work of David Smith for the first time, an encounter which is usually identified as the seismic moment when Caro abandons the clay and bronze figurative sculpture of

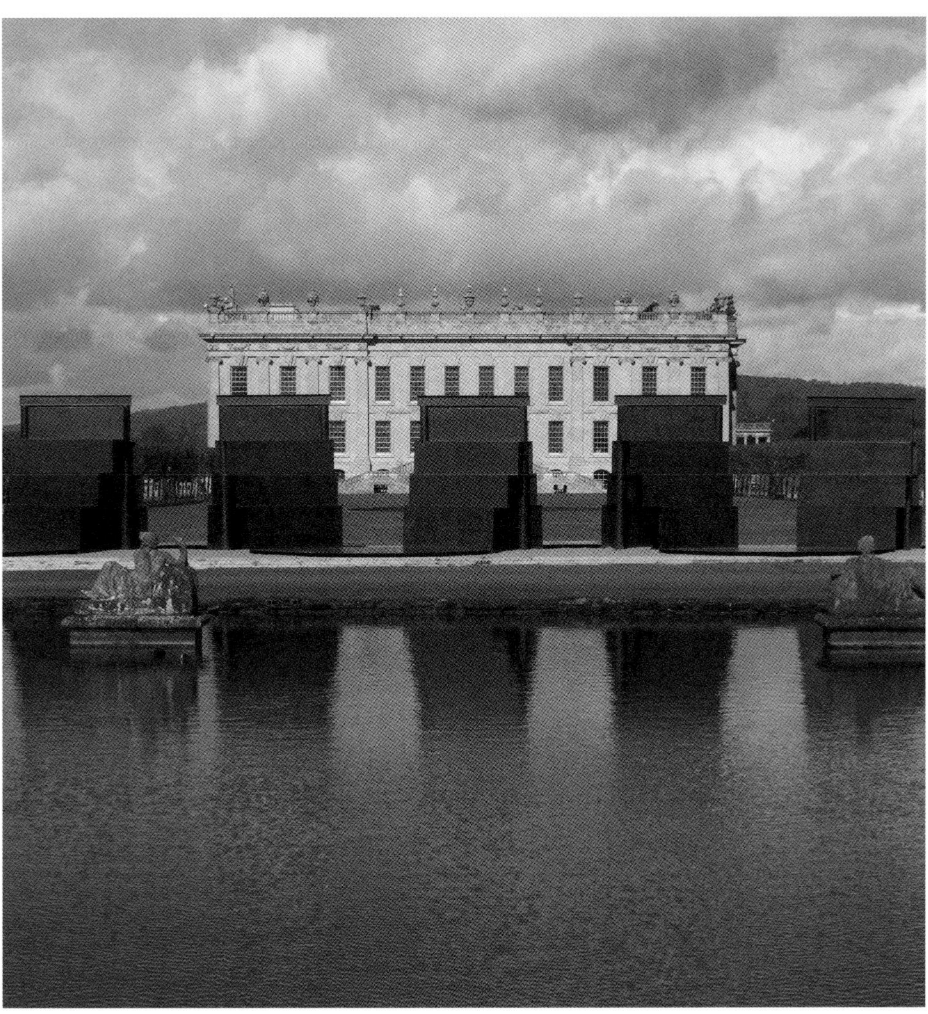

Anthony Caro, *Goodwood Steps* (1994–96) in *Caro at Chatsworth* in 2012. Photo: Gautier Deblonde

his youth for abstract sculpture in steel. Moore and Smith are therefore presented as polar opposites within the trajectory of Caro's development as an artist. But despite the great differences between them, the two sculptors are connected by a shared preoccupation with showing their respective work in the landscape, specifically the grounds around their studios. So in fact, by continually repeating his stance on the advantages of showing sculpture indoors, we can see how Caro was disassociating himself from the work of both Moore and Smith and thereby forging his own position.

Towards the end of his career Caro pointed out that 'the best thing to do, if you don't want to go the Henry Moore route, if you make a sculpture for outside, is go like a house: make it more like a house, make it oppose the countryside, not be part of it'.[4] This interest in the relationships between sculpture and architecture was realised in a series of epic works which he called 'sculpitecture'; *Sea Music* is one of the first attempts to fuse together the two separate disciplines. *Goodwood Steps* (1994), for example, is one of a number of subsequent 'stepped' works, of which two –

Halifax Steps (1994) and *Millbank Steps* (2004) – were originally conceived and shown inside. *Millbank Steps* formed the centrepiece of Caro's retrospective at Tate in 2005 and is now on show outside in the sculpture park at Roche Court. The Steps series are Caro at his most architectural; arguably, though, it is only when they are seen in the landscape that can most convincingly be regarded as sculptures. Whilst the viewer can enter inside their cathedral-like interior, it is really only by stepping back that it is possible to experience them fully and as objects. The same is true of *Sea Music*. It seems entirely appropriate for a sculptor like Caro, who has been preoccupied with the conception and representation of sculptural space, to show his work where there is enough space, beyond the confines of the gallery and unrestricted by walls, so that the viewer is able to experience it up close and from afar. Certainly, by taking sculpture off its traditional plinth in the 1960s, as he did with early works, Caro ensured it became part of the environment in which it is located and created an unmediated, intimate encounter. And as *Sea Music* demonstrates, this experience of his work is just as compelling when it happens outdoors.

Sea Music was unveiled on 22 November 1991.[5] Most striking amongst the facts of its birth – other than it involving no public money – is just how quickly this major project was realised. A site was selected, a model made and approved, and the sculpture was installed with what seems like comparative ease, largely due to the efforts of Tom Roberts (then Borough architect and chair of Poole Arts Council) and the support readily received from a forward-thinking Poole Borough Council.[6] Local businesses donated the time, materials and expertise whilst Caro demanded and was given full creative freedom.

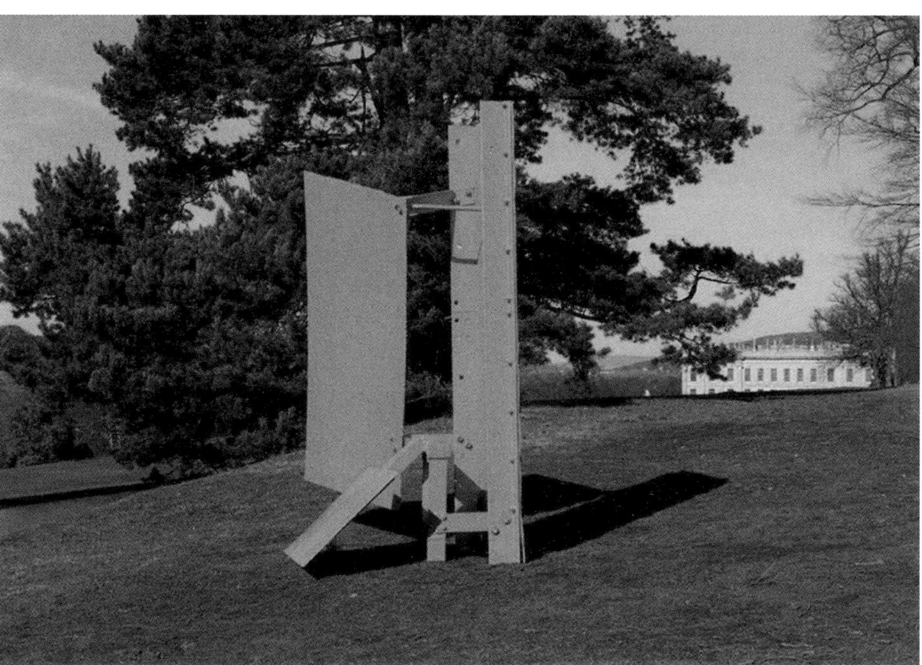

Anthony Caro, *Capital* (1960) in *Caro at Chatsworth* in 2012. Photo: Gautier Deblonde

Caro thought about the 'right' kind of sculpture very carefully, considering both modern Poole and its noble maritime history. In his account of the process, Caro states that he felt the site necessitated an 'open, free work, airy and fresh… a meeting point of town and harbour'. He very much wanted the sculpture to play an important part in everyday life:

> I was keen to involve the inhabitants and visitors to Poole in the experience of the sculpture by incorporating walkways to give people better views of the harbour. There would be new places to sit and enjoy the view which is superb and at the same time there would be an involvement with the sculpture. It would be almost as if people were up there within it, rather like being on the crow's nest of a sailing ship.

He also stated that he wanted *Sea Music* to evoke both the sound and appearance of the cascading sea, which he achieved through interlocking rings and curves, whilst the central vertical plate recalls the masts and sails of tall ships.

He further noted: 'I sometimes think of sculpture like a concerto: there's the piano up above and the orchestra down below.' It is perhaps no surprise that *Sea Music* resembles a treble clef and one certainly feels a sense of rhythm and movement whilst looking at the sculpture. Music was important to Caro. His assistants recall how Caro would ask them to select music from his vast collection, which would be played daily in the studio, almost – but not quite – drowning out the cacophony of welding and cutting steel. As a theme, music is also

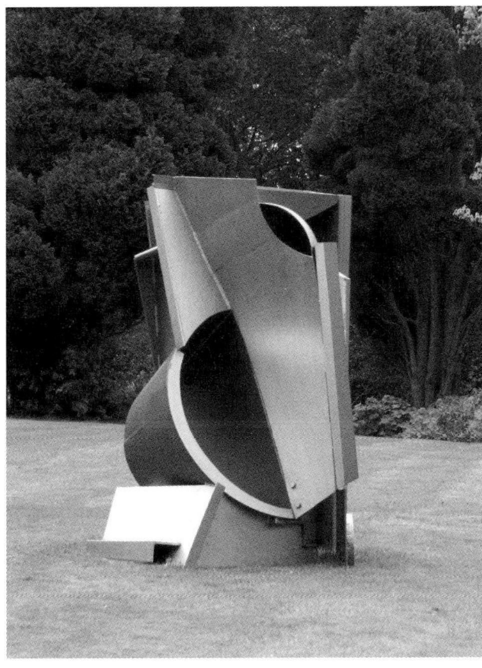

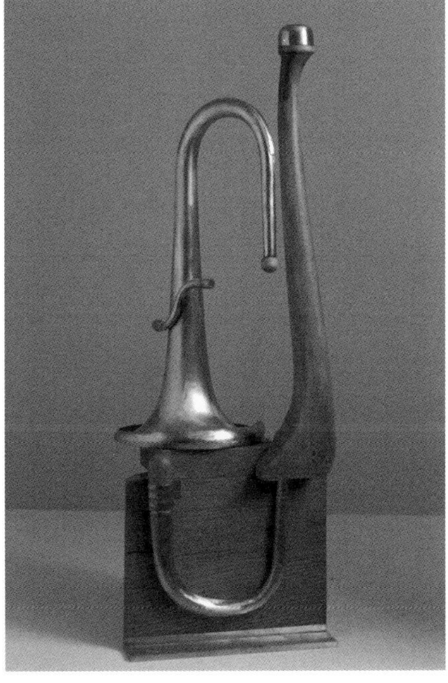

Anthony Caro, *Slow March* (1985) in the sculpture park at the New Art Centre, Roche Court.

Anthony Caro, *Double Bass* (Concerto series) (1999)

associated with a number of works. Titles such as *Slow March* (1985) are evocative of the heavy, sonorous movements of a military band, whilst found elements from actual musical instruments have been incorporated in the Concerto series (1999–2000). This group of works were made in Caro's studios in London and Dorset and emerged around the time he had been working on a large narrative work called *The Last Judgement* (1995–99), for which he wanted to incorporate some trumpet shapes in a section appropriately named *The Last Trump*. Coincidentally, Dave Thomas who supplied Caro with welding supplies at the time, also played in a brass band; he knew somebody who repaired instruments and could provide the necessary parts.

In 2013, Michael Spender from Poole Museum approached Caro about *Sea Music* as the sculpture was badly in need of conservation after more than twenty years in situ on the sea front; weather, salty sea air, seagulls and vandalism had all taken their toll and the sculpture was in danger of deteriorating beyond repair.[7] This resulted in a project generously supported by the Heritage Lottery Fund and Arts Council England, which has ensured that the sculpture is structurally sound for years to come and will also enhance its appearance. Caro felt it was an opportunity to help differentiate, through the use of paint, the actual sculpture from the main architectural elements. Shortly before he died, Caro approached me to help oversee the project, stating his hope that the conservation was also an opportunity to increase awareness of the sculpture, and to place it within his oeuvre as a major example of his work, crucial to his overall enduring reputation. The latter aspect became even more important following Caro's death in the autumn of 2013.

Working closely with Poole Museum and Caro's studio and a large number of local partners has ensured Caro's wishes have been carried out. In addition, funding has allowed a number of other activities to take place. Aside from the actual conservation, a long-term management and maintenance plan for *Sea Music* has been drawn up, the area around the sculpture has been improved and new lighting installed. An interpretation programme that re-engages the community of Poole with the piece and introduces a wider audience to the experience and understanding of this unique work has also begun. This is the first time *Sea Music* has been brought into such focus and this book commemorates these combined efforts. It also marks special events marking the relaunch of the sculpture including the exhibition of Caro's Concerto series in Poole Museum and the siting of his *Slow March* sculpture outside on the museum's terrace. David Ward has photographed *Sea Music* before, during and after conservation and his work illustrates this book and is also displayed in the museum. Finally, the contemporary classical composer Jim Aitchison has been commissioned to write a piece in response to *Sea Music*, including a 'fanfare for Caro' which heralds its relaunch.[8] The conservation is indeed something to welcome: it is an opportunity to start celebrating Caro's sculpture as a unique public commission, one that encourages a sense of ownership and pride in the work amongst the Dorset residents and inspires new visitors alike.

1 'Sculpture into Song' was realised by Michael Armstrong (SoundStorm Music Education Agency), Emma Kerr (Roche Court Educational Trust) and Katie Sayles (musician) with support from The D'Oyly Carte Charitable Trust.

2 Phyllis Tuchman, 'An interview with Anthony Caro', *Artforum*, no.10, June 1972, p.56.

3 Ian Barker, *Anthony Caro: Quest for a New Sculpture*, Swiridoff Verlag, Künzelsau, 2004, p.94.

4 Martina Droth, exhibition catalogue, *Caro at Chatsworth*, New Art Centre, East Winterslow, 2012, p.13.

5 *Sea Music* was given to Poole by the artist and made, without public money, by Bourne Steel Ltd and Burt & Vick Ltd. Additional help was given by The Angle Ring Bending Company; Joseph Ash; Brixey Engineering Ltd; British Steel; D'Angibau & Malim; Walker Hinds; Grayston White & Sparrow Ltd; Herberts; Newton Steel Stock; The Mansion House, Poole; and Wessex Water. The architect was Tom Roberts and the engineer was Derrick Robinson. The sculpture is owned by Poole Borough Council. It was unveiled by Lord Palumbo, then chairman of the Arts Council of Great Britain.

6 Poole Arts Council was a voluntary organisation formed in 1988. At the time *Sea Music* was originally commissioned, it comprised Tom Roberts (Chairman); John Bowen (Vice Chair); Brian Bone (Treasurer); Jenny Surridge (Secretary); Mary Granger; Roy Hall; Graham Parsons; and Frank Turland. The patrons were Anthony Caro; Hugh Casson and Elisabeth Frink; and subsequently John Hubbard and John Makepeace. It ran until mid-2000 and was no longer listed with the Charity Commission by 2009.

7 The conservation report was written by Jane Foley of Foley Conservation and the conservation work was carried out by Hall Conservation Ltd.

8 The contemporary composer Jim Aitchison was commissioned to write *Sea of Music*, a new piece of music inspired by *Sea Music* and particular music Caro liked, including Brahms's Fourth Symphony, Mozart's Piano Concerto no.20 and Schubert's String Quintet in C. Aitchison's new piece formed part of a concert marking the unveiling of the conserved sculpture, performed by Bournemouth Symphony Orchestra's Kokoro ensemble.

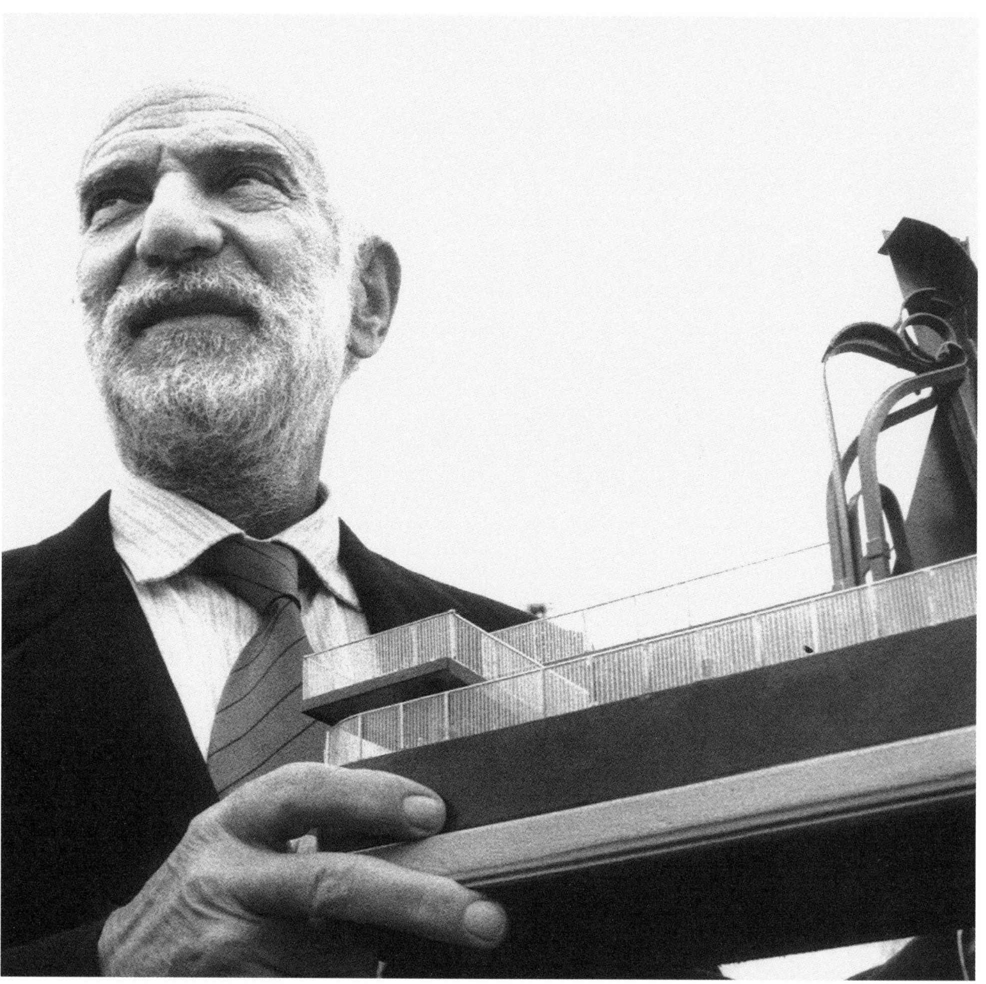

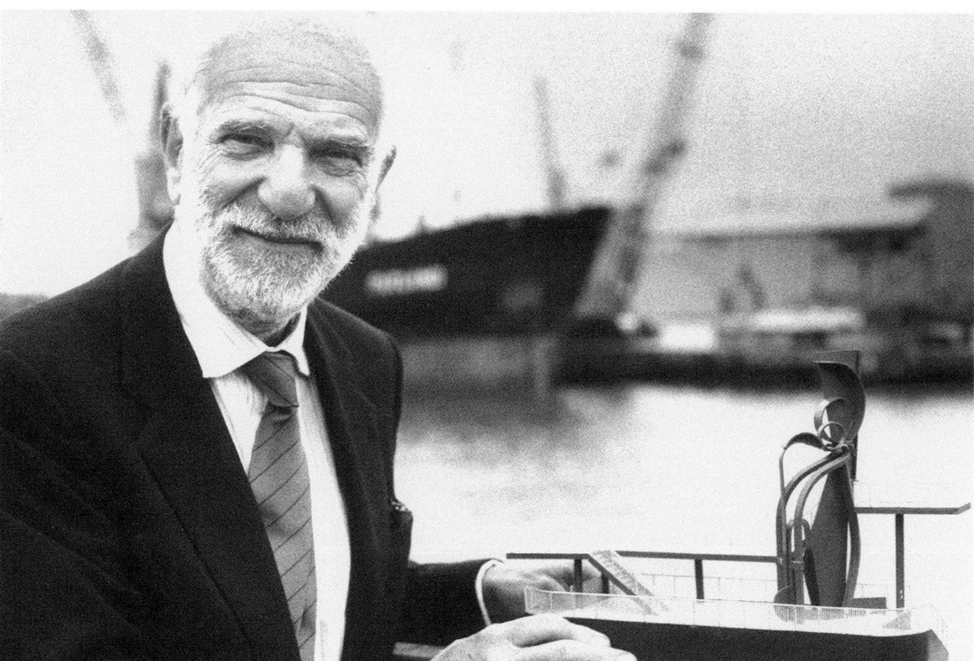

Anthony Caro with the model of *Sea Music*, 16 September 1991. Photo: Hattie Miles/ *Bournemouth Daily Echo*

Sir Anthony Caro Recalls: Sea Music

Anthony Caro

Tom Roberts made a telephone call to me out of the blue. I had not met him but he was full of enthusiasm about the idea of a sculpture or 'sculpitecture' on the Quay at Poole. After Tom's telephone call in summer 1989, we visited the proposed site near the Lifeboat Museum and started considering possibilities for this place. It meant making a scale model of the site, with the Lifeboat Museum about two feet long. This scale model was taken down to Worth Matravers where Pat Cunningham and I were joined by Tom Roberts to construct and try out possible suggestions of maquettes for the site. It seemed a good idea to start from existing table pieces and so we made about a dozen paper and cardboard models and in the end selected two as most likely. However, this site was subsequently rejected by the Harbour Master as it was used by the fishermen; and so another site on the Quay, the Pumping Station, was chosen.

Working from a large Catalan table piece we began to make a half-size scale model in the studio in London. This got to be so big that we found it was very hard to grasp it; it was too tall for the studio and making the parts was so complex that it slowed our procedure down. There was too much engineering in making the model, for example curving the post elements was in itself a two-week job, so making changes became very hard and unnatural. I decided instead to make the model third scale. Pat, Simon and I went back to Poole to look at the new site and to try to resolve the sort of size that the final sculpture should be. We met Tom there and using surveyor's measuring sticks, began to get a feel for the scale of the parts in relation to the surroundings, i.e. ship masts, crane booms etc. The site called for an open, free work, airy and fresh. It needed to be a strong punctuation point to give a focus to the High Street, a meeting point of town and harbour. The sculpture had to have the feel of the sea, of waves breaking, as well as of the harbour, masts and the sails of ships. At the same time, I was keen to involve the inhabitants and visitors to Poole in the experience of the sculpture by incorporating walkways to give people better views of the harbour. There would be new places to sit and enjoy the view which is superb and at the same time there would be an involvement with the sculpture. It would be almost as if people were up there within it, rather like being on the crow's nest of a sailing ship.

At Poole we found ourselves responding to existing bollards on the Quay and similar objects which I felt could be echoed in the sculpture. Being open to the public and without the personal control of attendants it was necessary to build the walkways and stairways in accordance with Building Control legislation. Tom designed them in association with me and the Structural Engineer, Derrick Robinson, who oversaw the overall safety of the structure. At this stage I brought in our model maker, Alec Vassiliades, to make a 1/50th model of the sculpture and proposed walkways.

In the meantime we continued with our third-size model in steel, which was about ten feet high. We built this on the floor of the studio and tried to make it a good sculpture, at the same time bearing in mind how the enlargement would relate to the setting. By this stage we had made many big alterations, and Alec had made yet another model on the very small scale. The tiny model helped me to clarify my ideas about the full-size work and many changes got made because I could visualise the scale more easily on the tiny model. This all took about six months working solely on this sculpture. Next we had Eamon Devlin, a carpenter, come in and, working from Tom's drawings, he built a model of the Pumping Station which was also a third in size. To this we fitted railings and walkways and placed our third model on it and adjusted the walkways to suit. We decided it would clarify the view of the sculpture if we slightly simplified the design of the Pumping Station and to this end we adjusted the design of the existing curved walls and staircases.

Alec then took the small-scale model and made an entire model of the High Street and the quayside illustrating the environmental context. The whole thing was then put onto a stand 1.5 metres high so that we could show this to Members of Poole Borough Council. The Mayor and Councillors, accompanied by Alasdair Ferguson, came to my studio and were shown both the third-scale model, on which we had placed some figures to give more sense of scale, plus the small-scale model of the town – together with photographs of Poole Harbour. After a pleasant lunch we were happy that the Mayor and Councillors felt it would be a good thing to go ahead. Visits to my studio were then arranged for David Sands (Managing Director of Bourne Steel), Derrick Robinson (an Engineer from Poole Borough Council), a Director from Angle Ring Co and Mike Dobson from British Steel.

Later we had the model taken down to Poole to Bourne Steel; and computer-generated survey drawings were made of it by the Engineer. Pat and I paid a couple of visits to Bourne Steel to check on progress, but everything seemed to us to be being done extremely well and the problems were clearly being met in an efficient and sensitive way. Pat made visits to check out sizes, joints, pipes, etc., and to iron out some of the practical problems, keeping in touch with the fabrication of this very large structure. Its galvanising and painting had to be of the highest specification to ensure protection to the surface for five to ten years.

We had some problems deciding on the colour and in fact it had to be mixed and made up especially by a paint company to get it exactly right. Our main involvement with the sculpture recommenced as soon as it arrived on the Quay. We visited to supervise the erection of the parts as they were manoeuvred into place by crane. This was done with accuracy and care. In fact, all the operations were done with a background of great goodwill and good feeling. As I suspected, certain changes were needed to make the sculpture look stronger against the sky. We made these alterations, but working on such big steel parts necessitated long delays. Cutting metal two inches thick, hoisting and welding each piece takes a long time and many hours and even days passed as each element was put together. At the time of writing the sculpture itself is in position and is being welded up stronger to withstand the force of the winds. It will then get its final coat of paint which will provide the finishing colour and protection against rust and deterioration in this salty and wet environment.

On Monday we will be there again to witness the placement of the walkways and staircases. On 22 November, we will all attend the opening by Lord Palumbo, Chairman of the Arts Council of Great Britain.

8 November 1991

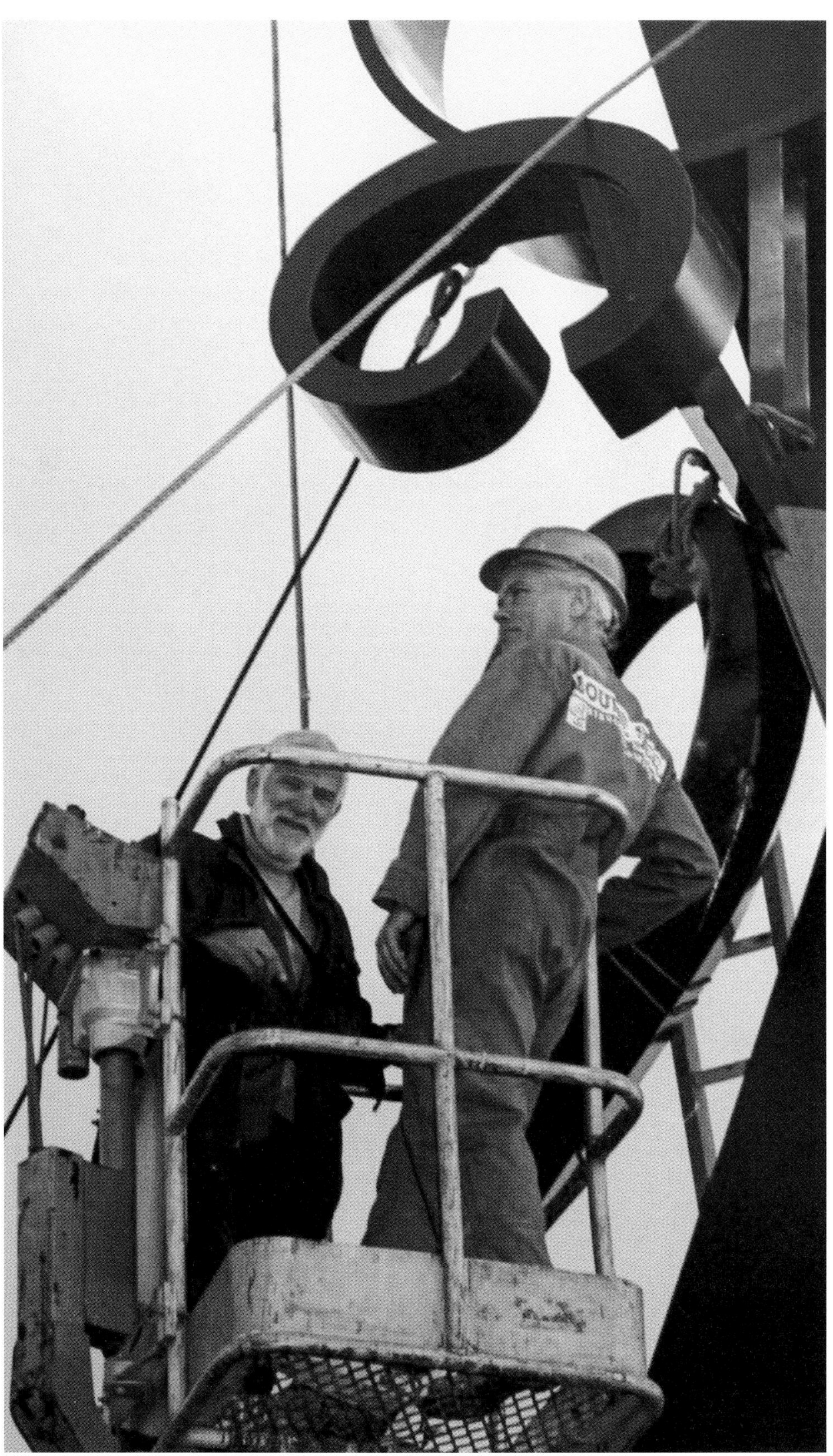

Anthony Caro during the installation of *Sea Music*, October 1991.
Photo: *Bournemouth Daily Echo*

The Story of Sea Music

Alistair Sooke

A little after midday on 22 November 1991, Lord Palumbo, then chairman of the Arts Council of Great Britain, smashed a bottle against the midnight-blue flank of *Sea Music*, a new, large-scale sculpture created by Anthony Caro especially for Poole in Dorset, and given to the town by the artist. It was a ceremonial act, 'launching' the 37-foot-high sculpture as though she were a ship – appropriately enough, given the maritime setting, as well as the work's nautical associations: 'The sculpture had to have the feel of the sea, of waves breaking, as well as of the harbour, masts and the sails of ships', Caro had explained, shortly before the official unveiling. The ceremony marked the culmination of more than two years of effort by Caro as well as local businesses, benefactors and enthusiasts, many of whom had volunteered materials, time and expertise. Chief among them was Tom Roberts, then head of the Borough of Poole's Design, Architecture and Environment Unit and the chairman of the town's voluntary arts council, who had cold-called Caro in 1989, planting the seed that would eventually flourish as *Sea Music*.

Amid the fanfare, as Palumbo spoke before television cameras and members of the regional and national press, there was an atmosphere of optimism. Thanks to Roberts's determination and diplomacy, a seaside town had persuaded a recently knighted artist of international significance to create what remains – unbelievably – his only monumental, site-specific and permanent public sculpture in Britain. It was a coup. With only a little irony, a press release announced that *Sea Music* was Poole's 'answer to the Statue of Liberty'.

Admittedly, some townspeople were disgruntled: there were mutterings in the *Poole Advertiser* that *Sea Music* was 'revolting' and 'diabolical'. A few inhabitants joked

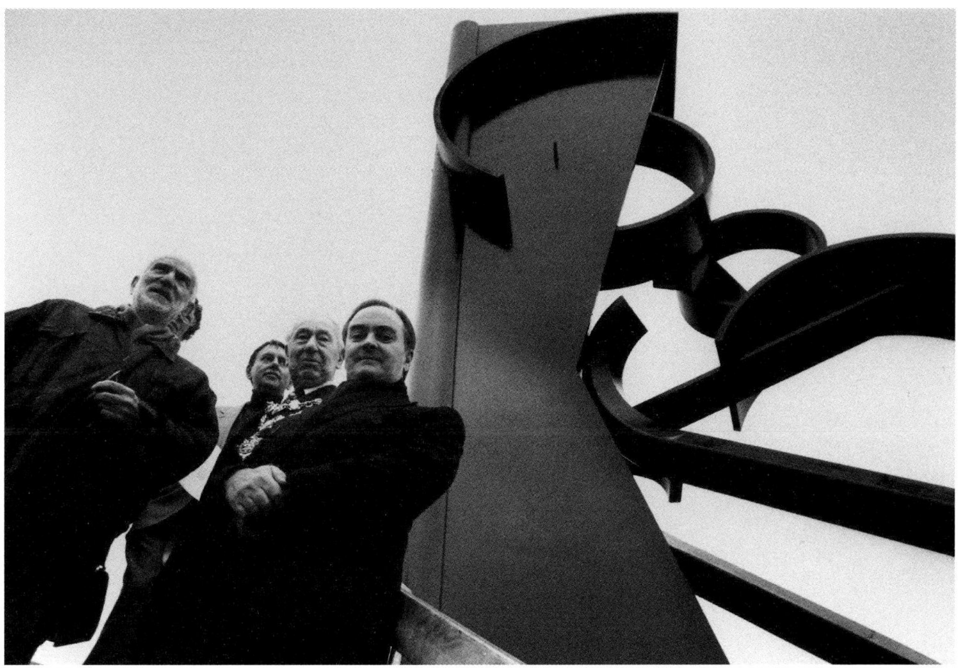

The launch of *Sea Music* on 22 November 1991: Anthony Caro with Lord Palumbo, Edward Hogg (then Mayor of Poole) and Tom Roberts. Photo: Hattie Miles/ *Bournemouth Daily Echo*

that it resembled a can opener. Yet, from the outset, long before the design of *Sea Music* had been finalised, Caro anticipated this sort of reaction. 'When the sculpture is made and erected, that is when there may be some objections, because people do tend to object to sculptures', he wrote to Roberts on 14 May 1990. 'But people generally in the end tend to grow to like their works of art in their towns and cities.'

Poole's leaders echoed his equanimity. *Sea Music* had been built for an estimated £130,000, at no cost to the public. It was a gift that would surely prove a major asset for the town. At its peak, during the eighteenth century, when the fisheries trade was booming, Poole had been one of the busiest ports in Britain. *Sea Music* was going to put Poole back on the map. Besides, anyone who did not like the sculpture could at least use its observation platforms to enjoy a magnificent panorama of the harbour. In the years that followed, Caro himself often did just that, sitting on one of the platforms with his wife, the painter Sheila Girling, while enjoying a simple meal of fish and chips. As he once said about *Sea Music*, 'It [was] almost as if people were up there within it, rather like being on the crow's nest of a sailing ship.' *Sea Music* isn't a sculpture to be looked at, you see, so much as experienced.

Twenty-five years after it was unveiled, I visited Poole to see how *Sea Music* had fared. The controversy that once engulfed it had abated, as Caro predicted it would, but *Sea Music* was suffering from exposure to a different sort of adversity: namely, the wet, salty climate. Weathering had damaged the viewing platforms surrounding the sculpture, discolouring the galvanised steel railings and the

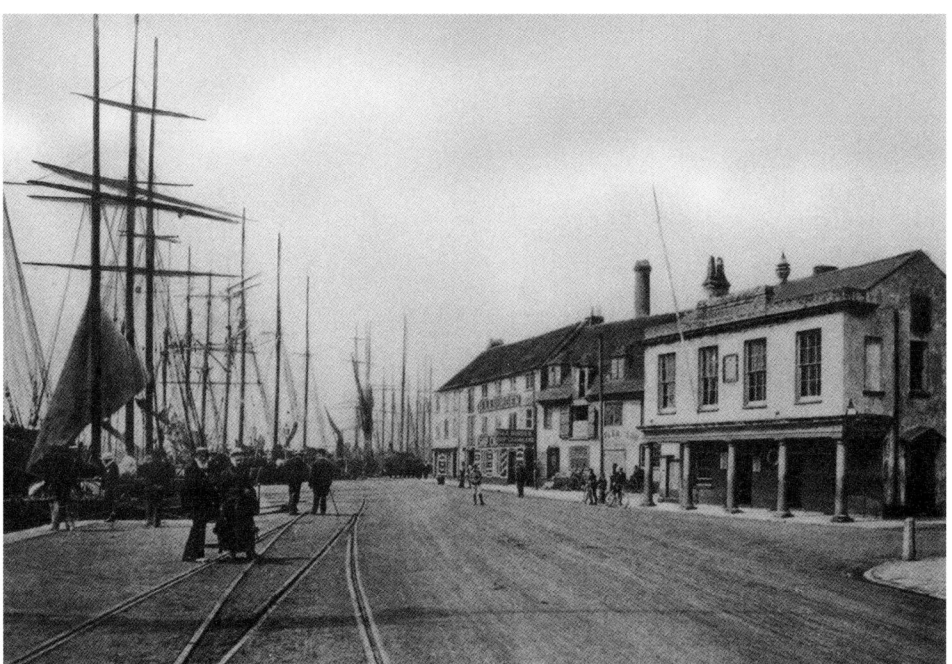

Image of historic Poole from Caro's *Sea Music* archives.

wooden seats and decking, and severely rusting the furniture's iron fittings. The brackish environment had also begun to corrode the sculpture itself so that its structure was in danger of becoming unsafe. Roosting pigeons and seagulls had taken their toll, graffiti had been sprayed down a vertical plane of the sculpture, and nearby streetlights and municipal signs cluttered the site. With its lyrical flourishes and swooping, thrusting forms, *Sea Music* had once embodied a mood of optimism and civic pride. Over time, though, the sculpture had become befogged with melancholy and neglect.

All this, of course, has been reversed, thanks to the Heritage Lottery Fund. But something else struck me on my visit to Poole, and that was how the sculpture's sad condition offered a metaphor for the way it has been perceived – not only locally, but nationally and internationally too – until now. Contrast Caro's career, for a moment, with that of Henry Moore, whom he assisted in the early 1950s. Public sculptures by Moore are, if not ubiquitous, then very common in Britain. Yet Caro, the dominant sculptor of the generation following Moore, made just one major outdoor work for his homeland. This fact alone should ensure that *Sea Music* is cherished and celebrated far beyond the limits of Poole. Yet, even within the art world, it is still not widely known. Everyone is familiar with the graceful painted-steel sculptures that Caro created during the radical breakthrough years of the 1960s. Most of his later achievements, though, remain underappreciated. Within the extensive literature written about Caro, there are only scant references to *Sea Music* and next to nothing in terms of prolonged analysis or discussion. This is not to say that *Sea Music* is despised or discounted so much as forgotten and overlooked. It is, as it were, there but not there, with none of the stellar profile of later, better-known works of public art, such as Antony Gormley's *Angel of the North* (1998), which it arguably heralded. This indifference to *Sea Music* is, I believe, both sad and wrong. So, in the hope of raising awareness about the magnitude of this important sculpture, this essay will tell its history in full, as straightforwardly as possible, for the first time.

Since nothing substantial has been written about *Sea Music*, I have relied upon two sources: Patrick Cunningham, Caro's principal studio assistant from 1969 and more recently his studio director, who was involved with the genesis and fabrication of *Sea Music* at every stage (and who has participated in its conservation), and the archives at Barford Sculptures, the artist's studio in London. Most of the documents relating to *Sea Music* consist of correspondence between Caro and Roberts. As well as forming the spine of the narrative of the sculpture's creation, these letters reveal the prominence of Roberts's role within the story. Reading them, it becomes obvious that Caro depended upon Roberts for everything from raising money and support for *Sea Music* to navigating the administrative labyrinth that led to securing planning permission for it. Caro also agreed to Roberts's designs for the surrounding walkways and staircases, down to the railings and seating. Above all, Roberts shouldered the burden of practical concerns, providing Caro with the freedom to create.

On 8 November 1991, Caro sat down to record his memories of how the sculpture had come about. 'Tom Roberts made a phone call to me out of the blue', he began. That telephone conversation must have occurred in early June 1989, because soon afterwards, on the twelfth of that month, Roberts, in his capacity as chairman of Poole Arts Council, followed up with a formal letter to Caro. In it, he said that he would be 'delighted' to meet 'one weekend soon to talk about the idea of an environmental project in Poole'. He continued: 'As an architect very interested in such issues, I am endeavouring to bring together a small group of eminent architects and sculptors to address the idea of an environmental project – something of building scale which is a statement about the quality of a specific urban space and its unique location. Poole Quay could be a good location.' At this early stage, then, Roberts was thinking only in general terms. He planned to invite several artists and architects – not just Caro – to propose 'environmental projects' for Poole Quay. Still, calling Caro was an enterprising move. Roberts was aware of the artist's personal connection with the area: Caro periodically spent weekends and holidays with his family at an old coastguard's cottage, with a studio, which he owned on St Aldhelm's Head on the Dorset coast.

Not long after Roberts had sent this initial letter, he met Caro in Poole to look at the site he had in mind: a location by the old lifeboat station at the east end of the Quay. 'Sir Anthony and I spent a delightful afternoon wandering around Poole and

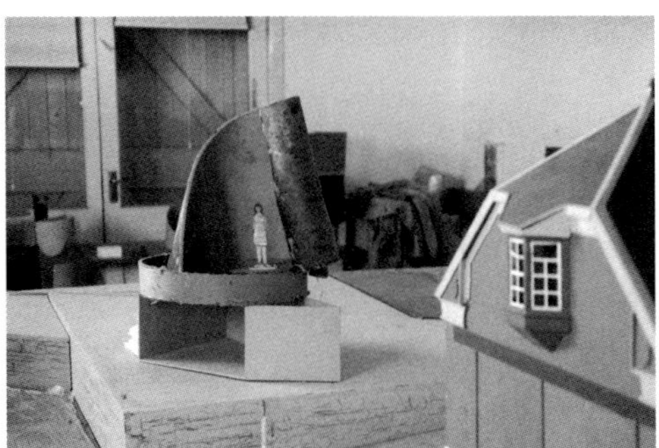

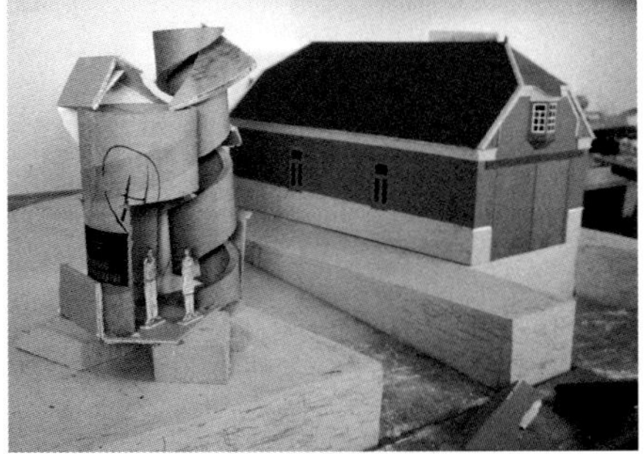

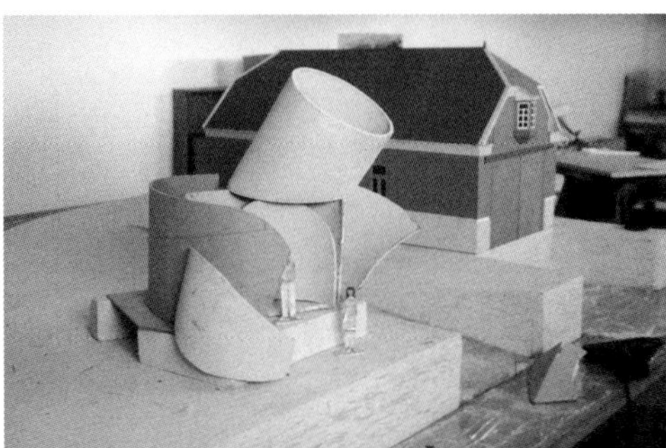

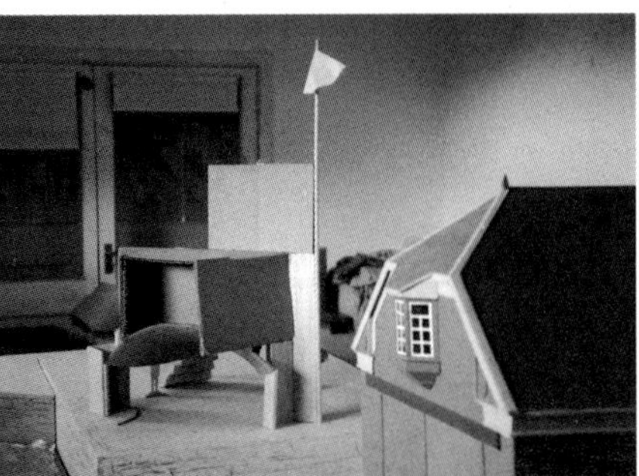

Some of the maquettes considered for the site near the lifeboat station in Poole.

enthusiastically talking about the atmosphere, which we both felt was unique', he recalled. Attracted to the 'splendid vista' of the 'summer scene' before him, as Caro later put it, 'dominated by sea and sky, yacht masts and sails fluttering', the artist felt excited about the possibilities. He commissioned a scale model of the site, including a two-foot-long replica of what he called the 'Lifeboat Museum'. He then took this model to his cottage and invited Roberts and Cunningham to join him. The point of the meeting was, he later explained, 'to construct and try out possible suggestions of maquettes for the site. It seemed a good idea to start from existing table pieces and so we made about a dozen paper and cardboard models and in the end selected two as most likely.' A group of unlabelled colour photographs in Caro's archives documents this part of the process. The backdrop is a room in Caro's cottage. In the foreground, next to a model of a red building that is immediately recognisable as Poole's old lifeboat station, several cardboard maquettes are presented from different angles. They are all models for 'table pieces', i.e. small-scale sculptures, designed to be displayed on a table top, which Caro had been producing since the mid-1960s. However, none of the maquettes, which at that stage were experimenting with box-like structures and hefty cylinders, yet anticipated the final design of *Sea Music*.

Caro presented a version of one of these models at the first arts festival organised by Poole Arts Council on the weekend of 30 September and 1 October 1989. Roberts wrote a short text to accompany the display of Caro's 'conceptual idea' for a new work developed for Poole Quay. Entitled 'Big Art: Anthony Caro', it suggested another reason why Roberts was interested in the artist, aside from his personal connection with the area. As an architect, Roberts was intrigued by the

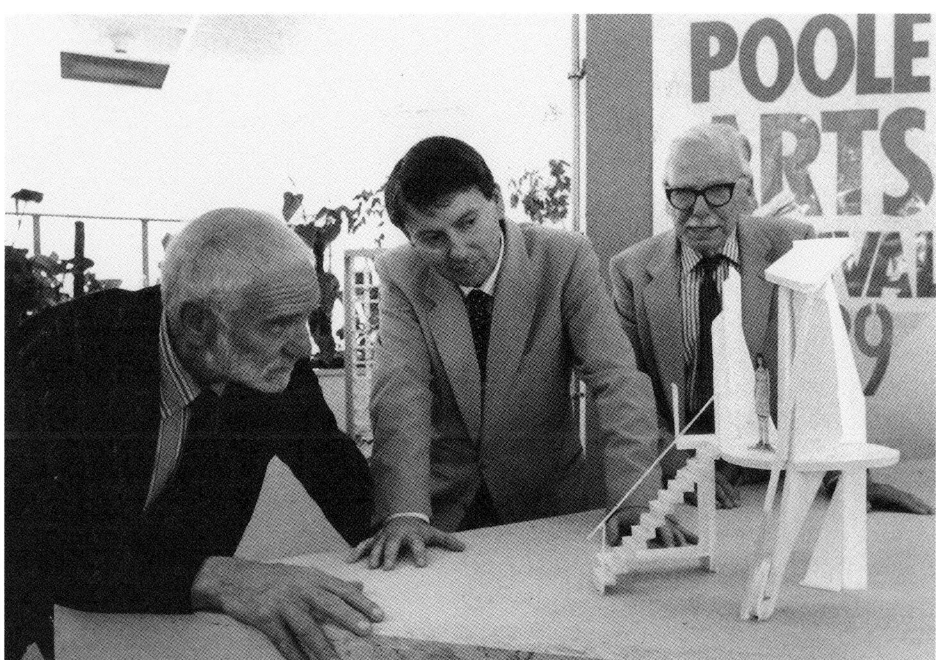

Anthony Caro and Tom Roberts with the maquette made for the first arts festival in Poole in 1989. Photo: *Bournemouth Evening Echo*

directions in which Caro's work had been moving during the 1980s, specifically his exploration of the relationship between sculpture and architecture. This shift in his work towards what Caro later called, in a somewhat ungainly coinage, 'sculpitecture', culminated in the large *Tower of Discovery*, which was made for his exhibition at the Tate Gallery, *Sculpture Towards Architecture*, in 1991. The same text continued to explain how Caro was 'expanding the scale of his work on to an architectural level': 'He has moved away from the idea of sculpture as a closed object, which the spectator walks around and views at a respectful distance. Recent Caro projects in America and Britain have embraced space, inviting the spectator to enter and explore the structures. Forms suggest door openings, walls, windows, stairs, terraces and look-out points.' *Sea Music*, of course, subsequently integrated several of these architectural features.

By 14 December, Caro had finessed his 'thoughts about the sculpture for Poole', as he put it in a letter to Roberts. By this point, Roberts was trying to build support within Poole Borough Council for the idea of commissioning Caro to create an actual sculpture, rather than merely a 'conceptual idea' for one, on the town's historic quayside. He asked Caro to write a short statement outlining preliminary thoughts for what form such a sculpture could take, ahead of a meeting with Ian Andrews, Poole Borough Council's Town Clerk and Chief Executive. The statement survives. In it, Caro described a tall, 'airy' design, offset by a 'viewing platform' that would feel 'sturdy and firm'. 'Upright pole-like members would be countered by twisting ribbon-like plates', he wrote. 'I feel that steel painted or enamelled white would naturally relate to the boats, the gulls and the expanse of sky and water.' He concluded:

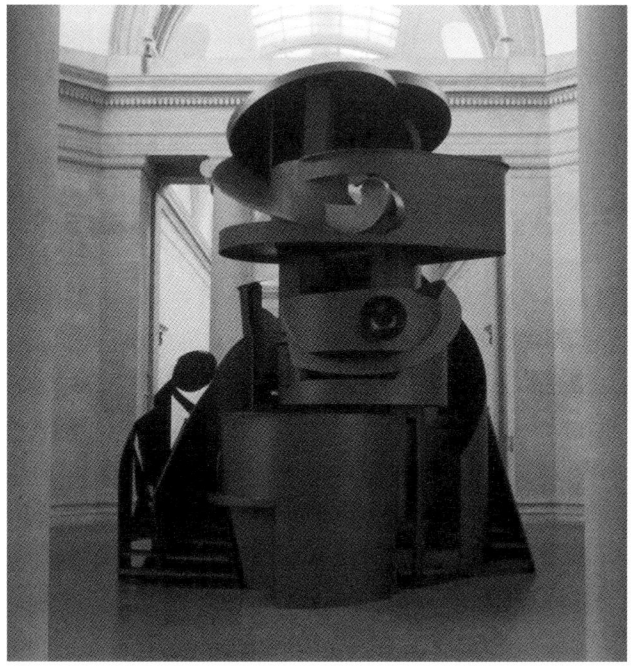

Anthony Caro, *Tower of Discovery* (1991) from the *Sculpture Towards Architecture* exhibition at the Tate Gallery.

> The sculpture would in no sense be a traditional monument or statue, it should rather be seen as a meeting point or celebration which hopefully would raise the spirits, as does the sight of the yachting and the water. As the Architect Utzon [sic] wrote about Sydney Opera House, 'you will never be finished with it – when you pass around it or see it against the sky … We know it as if we were sailing around it'. This also is my endeavour.

Roberts sent a copy of Caro's thoughts to Andrews, and arranged a meeting between the three of them for 28 January 1990.

A letter from Caro to Roberts, written just three days after this encounter, reveals that the meeting was a turning point in the sculpture's evolution. Aware that Poole's Harbour Commissioners would resist any proposal to erect a sculpture beside the lifeboat station, because the site was used by fishermen, Andrews and Roberts suggested another setting altogether, at the other, western end of the Quay. It was one that Caro had not considered, but, following the meeting, on his way back to London, he made a detour to inspect it, braving a 'gale' to do so. 'It is an interesting spot', he wrote, 'and it calls for a very different approach from the previous one.' Although the new 'spot', at the junction of the southern end of Poole's High Street ('a meeting point of town and harbour', as Caro later put it), was in a conservation area within the Old Town, which boasts several remarkable medieval buildings, it also encompassed an ugly pumping station – essentially a reinforced-concrete box owned by the utility company Wessex Water. But Caro liked the fact that the station provided a raised 'podium', i.e. a base, for the sculpture. He was also pleased that it was accessible by

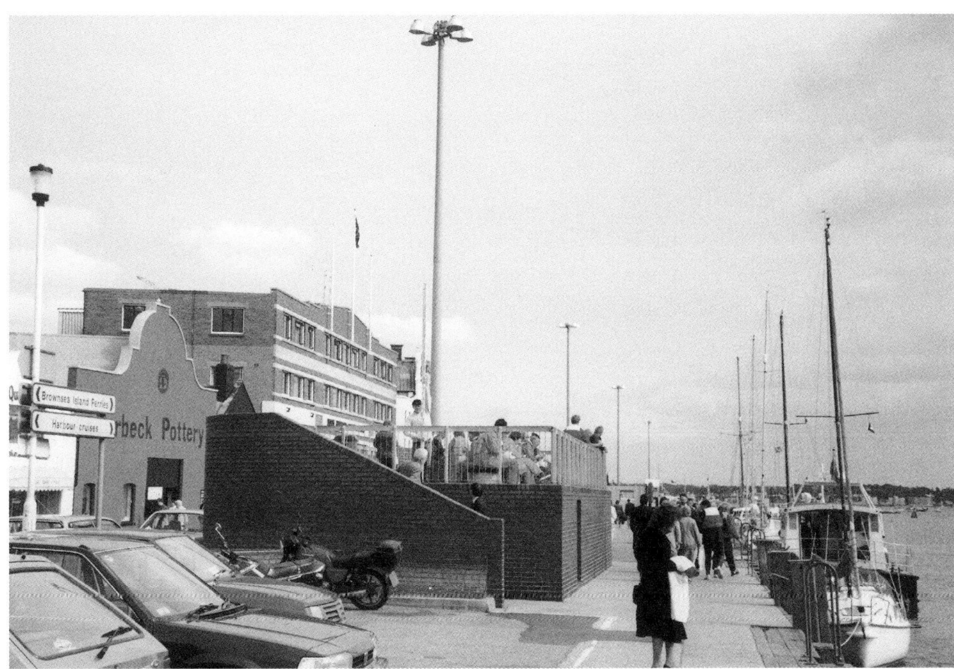

The final location chosen for the project on Poole Quay.

stairs – presumably because they offered possibilities for experiencing 'sculpitecture'. Moreover, he found himself responding to the heavier industry at the western end of the Quay, where fishing vessels could be seen, along with a vista of warehouses and busy shipyards bristling with cranes. All this transformed his vision for the sculpture: 'The fact that it's among different types of vessels implies a larger, heavier and more robust sculpture than that we were planning for the previous position (where I felt it should echo the masts, rigging and yachts).'

This letter, dated 31 January 1990, was important for another reason too. This was because it set out Caro's conditions for taking on the project. He offered to waive his fee ('in view of my association with Poole'), but, in return, Roberts would have to accept responsibility for every aspect of the project's 'financial side'. Caro also outlined a few specific practicalities: 'When I get the OK from you – I will embark on making a one half, or perhaps under the new circumstances a one third size model, in my studio. This model will belong to me on completion.' In the event, Caro stuck to this plan: the one-third-size model for *Sea Music*, on which he worked in London before it was later enlarged under his supervision by a steel company in Poole, was subsequently exhibited as a discrete sculpture called *Sea Adagio*. It is now in a private collection in Switzerland.

Because the wording of the 31 January letter was crucial, Caro was keen to get it right. He sent a draft to Ian Barker, a close associate and friend, accompanied by a short note, handwritten on his personal notepaper. In it, he set out three entirely sensible conditions before he could commit to the project: 'I'm willing to do the job providing (A) I have no more needless & fairly [sic] boring lunches with the

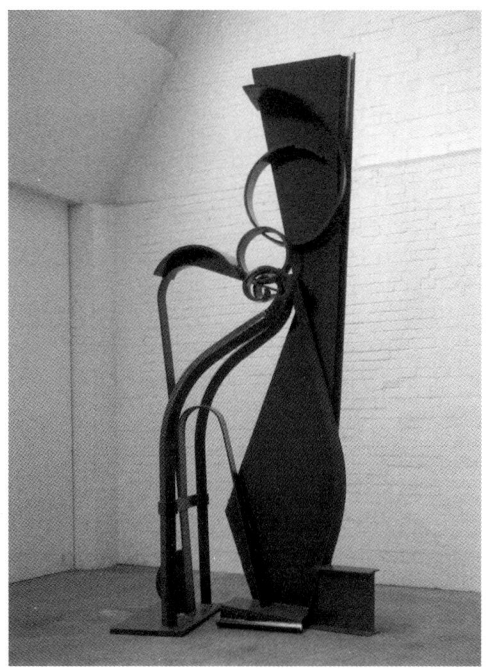

Anthony Caro,
Sea Adagio (1990–92)
Private Collection

Town Clerk etc etc (to try to convince them of the project!) or (B) no interference at all about the look of the sculpture or (C) no worry about costs or financial side of the project.' Caro was fond of Dorset, which, he said, restored his sanity after the madness of London. But, principally, he sensed a rare, perhaps even unprecedented, opportunity to work on a public sculpture of monumental scale entirely without interference. There would be no deferring to powerful patrons or decisions-by-committee; and, crucially, no worrying about the project's costs. He concluded his letter of 31 January by reiterating his central demand: 'It is important that I have freedom to make the final sculpture as I wish.'

Roberts acknowledged the terms of the artist's 'pact' – even if, as he wrote back, 'There are many hurdles to overcome.' From this moment, the project gathered pace. By the end of August 1990, planning permission for the sculpture had been achieved: 'This was a most unusual submission,' Roberts confided to Caro, 'the first in my experience where illustrations of the proposal were not available!' There was, however, a proviso: 'The Borough Council needs to agree the maquette before construction commences on site.' This, Roberts explained, was 'inevitable', although he did offer some reassurance: 'It is not the intention to interfere in any way with your design but is simply a practical way of overcoming the lack of substance at this moment in time.' He also reported that he had won approval from Wessex Water to use the pumping station as a 'podium' for the sculpture. Moreover, Bourne Steel, a local construction and engineering firm, had agreed to fabricate the finished work for free, and became the project's main sponsor. 'I can see no reason,' Roberts concluded, 'why we cannot now say to you "go ahead".' Caro's response was enthusiastic: 'I am amazed at the wonderful progress you have made!' he wrote, 'and I see no reason why we should not go ahead immediately. So much so that I have been twice to the Quay this weekend.' He also promised to have the model ready for the Borough Council 'by Christmas or soon after'.

Receiving the 'go ahead' reignited Caro's excitement about the project. He spent an evening on the Quay with his wife. 'I am getting the feel of the area very well', he told Roberts in early October, two days before the steel for the one-third-size model arrived at his studio in London. From this point on, though, there is little, if any, description of the model or its evolution in the trail of letters. Instead, Roberts and Caro corresponded about practical matters, such as the precise dimensions of the pumping station. Caro requested details about its weight-bearing capacity: 'We need to see how it is constructed inside as we will be putting quite a weight up there', he explained on 3 October. Eventually, a purpose-built steel frame was required to reinforce the pumping station. There was also a great deal of discussion about the design of the stairs and walkways, including the metalwork of the railings, which Caro entrusted to Roberts. On 7 January 1991, they spoke on the phone, and reached an important conclusion. Previously, there had been discussions about the walkways and how integrated with the sculpture they should be: at one point, in a letter to Roberts dated 14 May 1990, Caro had suggested that the brickwork and metal balustrade, which they were considering for the pumping station, should 'echo the feeling of the sculpture'. Certainly, Caro's term 'sculpitecture' implied the fusion of the two disciplines. Immediately after their conversation on 7 January, though, Caro wrote to Roberts from home, summarising his new position: 'I definitely do think that the walkways are architecture, architecture that passes through and passes by the sculpture, not integral to it ... And I don't think we ever really thought of the sculpture as having the horizontal walkways as a necessary integral part, though it was necessary to get this far in order to realise it.'

In the same letter, Caro included a sketch proposing the addition of a spiral staircase leading to an extra, even higher platform, like a crow's nest, which could accommodate three people. This, he explained, would accentuate the sculpture's appearance as a 'lookout tower' from the sea (from which perspective, he wrote, it appeared 'blanker' than from land). The sketch is significant because it reveals that, by this point, most of the fundamentals of *Sea Music* were in place. Caro's drawing emphasised the sculpture's tall, vertical central form, evoking perhaps a steamship's funnel, offset by a series of fluttering, curling strips of metal that almost bounced off it before cascading to the ground. The upper walkway sketched by Caro, meanwhile, supported by thin, upright, uncomplicated columns, was broadly in keeping with what was eventually constructed. The contrast, therefore, between the vertical sinuous sculpture, which was to play the starring role, and the supporting act of the horizontal straight walkways was paramount: 'I feel that one has to be strong and disciplined with the walkways and the uprights,' Caro wrote, '[and] leave the fluidity to the sculpture: otherwise we do get [an] art nouveau-look.' This was a reference to a recent memo, dated 27 December 1990, in which Roberts had sketched a possible design for the railings, incorporating an '(Art Nouveau) use of twisted bars'. Caro signed off his letter of 7 January with an exclamation of encouragement: 'Counting on you for the architecture side of it!'

By February, Roberts had enlisted the support of British Steel, who agreed to supply most of the raw materials for the sculpture at no cost. At a meeting in late February, Mike Dobson, a manager at British Steel, recommended 'mild steel with a paint finish' rather than Corten steel, because the latter would quickly look 'unsightly' when subjected to Poole's 'saline atmosphere' and 'bird excrement'. Roberts also sounded out Bourne Steel about a provisional fabrication schedule for the sculpture and walkways, beginning in May. 'The fog begins to lift and things become attainable', he wrote on 28 February to the Managing Director of the company. Upon seeing the complexity of the model for *Sea Music*, however, Bourne

Steel suggested delegating some of the more complicated work, such as bending the sculpture's secondary but still massive curved shapes and hollow sections, to a specialist firm elsewhere. Eventually, the Angle Ring Bending Company in Tipton, West Midlands, was used.

Of all the 'hurdles' that Roberts had foreseen, the biggest still had to be overcome: the visit to Caro's London studio of a delegation from Poole Borough Council to sign off the maquette before construction on the finished sculpture could commence. In the run-up to this important meeting, Caro recalled, he worked 'solely' on the one-third-size model for 'about six months'. His starting point was a recent table piece called *Catalan Double*, completed in 1988. In 1993, in a letter regarding an exhibition about *Sea Music* at Scaplen's Court in Poole the following year. Caro called *Catalan Double* the 'primary source' for *Sea Music*. He lent it to the exhibition, along with three other works from the Catalan series, and its importance is worth discussing here.

The Catalan series emerged after Caro convened an international workshop for painters and sculptors (one of the so-called 'Triangle Workshops' that he had initiated in 1982) in Barcelona in 1987. Working in the Catalan city for two and a half weeks, side-by-side with around fifty artists from all over the world, Caro explored the idea of 'drawing in sculpture'. He obtained quantities of curly steel scrap – including remnants of disused balconies and balustrades – and began a group of works that became known as the Barcelona sculptures. In London, the following year, he also started using smaller forged-steel parts from Spain to make the set of 33 table pieces to which *Catalan Double* belongs.

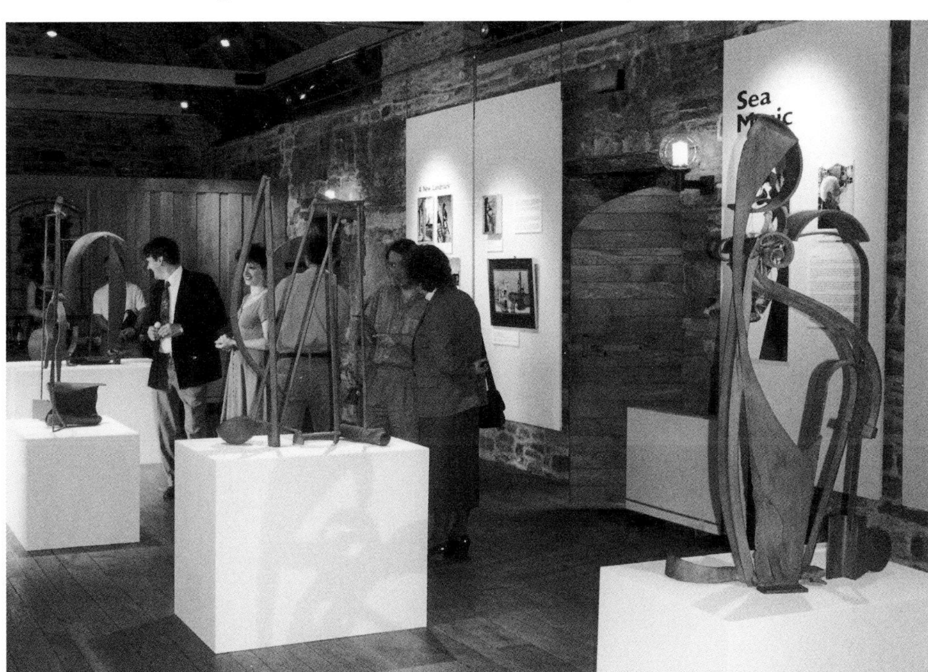

Sculptures from Caro's Catalan series in the exhibition *Sea Music: The Sculpture on Poole Quay* held at Scaplen's Court, Poole from 11 June – 24 July 1994.

Comparing *Catalan Double* with *Sea Music* is instructive, because Caro kept various elements of the former whilst also making significant changes. Two eye-catching 'rings', for instance, visible near the top of *Catalan Double*, remain essential elements in *Sea Music*. To Roberts, they called to mind 'whisps [sic] of vapour' emerging from a steamboat. Indeed, in general, the serpentine silhouette of *Sea Music* resembles that of *Catalan Double*, with all its curves and arabesques. Yet there is a significant difference between the two sculptures: the funnel-like blue plate at the centre of the larger work. The equivalent element in *Catalan Double* is much slighter and more graceful – it swoops and swerves, echoing the curling forms that surround it. While working on the model for *Sea Music*, Caro evidently decided to beef up this part, increasing its width to provide a greater impression of heft and solidity. This had a decisive impact because it repurposed *Catalan Double*, with all its associations of delicate, dancing Mediterranean metalwork, to suit the siting of *Sea Music* on a busy working harbour. 'At Poole we found ourselves responding to existing bollards on the Quay and similar objects which I felt could be echoed in the sculpture', Caro recalled. Bollards had caught his attention before: between 1982 and 1984, he had produced a series of massive sculptures using scrap steel from shipyards, including bollards as well as buoys. The central blue section of *Sea Music*, then, was meant to provide a strong, quasi-industrial, tower-like presence, ensuring that the sculpture would function as a landmark, readily seen from the other side of the harbour or out at sea. It was also supposed to conjure metaphorical associations appropriate for the setting: it could be part of a ship's bow, for instance, slicing through seawater represented by the other, more liquid forms, splashing up against it before flowing off to each side. Moreover, as well as a ship's funnel, it could

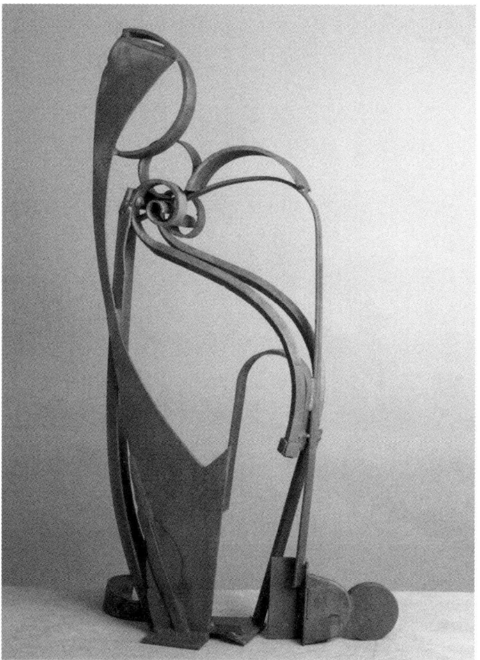

Anthony Caro, *Table Piece: Catalan Double* (1987–88) now in the collection of the Hessisches Landesmuseum, Darnstadt.

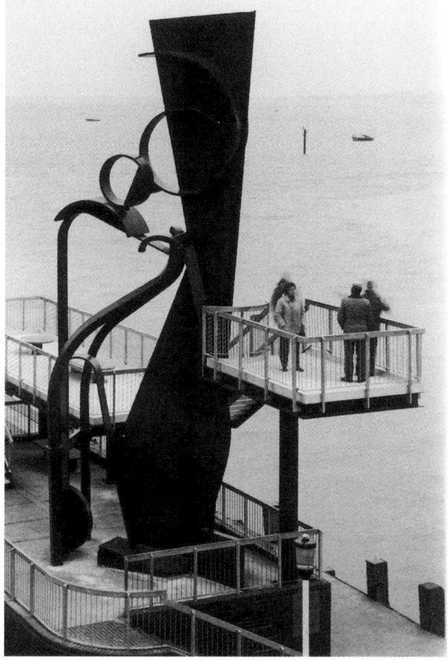

Sea Music, c.1991
Photo: Shigeo Anzai

evoke a sail, taut in the wind, surrounded by rigging – a reference, no doubt, to Poole's history, when the harbour was filled with sailboats rather than modern fishing vessels and pleasure craft. I am not suggesting that Caro wanted *Sea Music* – which is, after all, first and foremost an abstract sculpture – to be read in such a literal fashion. Still, the changes to *Catalan Double* that Caro made while working on the model for *Sea Music* were surely motivated by the suggestiveness of certain forms in a maritime context.

It was also during this period that the sculpture's title began to crystallise, after Caro noticed a resemblance between his model and a treble clef. In the past he had often used music as an analogy for the syncopated rhythms of his abstract sculptures. 'I sometimes think of sculpture like a concerto', he said. 'There's the piano up above and the orchestra down below.' Calling his new sculpture *Sea Music* ensured that it would appeal to the ear as well as the eye. Its title suggests that its buoyant three-dimensional forms represent the sound of sea, as well as the appearance of currents and waves breaking against the Quay.

One of the attractions for Caro of his London studio, a converted piano factory, was its size. Even so, working on an unwieldy model, which was itself more than 12 feet tall, proved to be slow-going. Eventually, the working model, which later became *Sea Adagio*, was placed on top of a wooden replica of the pumping station, to which Caro's assistants fitted railings and walkways, as well as figures to provide a sense of scale. Several black-and-white photographs record the impressive overall effect of this one-third-size rendering of *Sea Music*. In addition, Caro had a model made of Poole's Old Town with a small *Sea Music* in situ, so that when the councillors visited on 18 March 1991 they could understand 'the environmental context'.

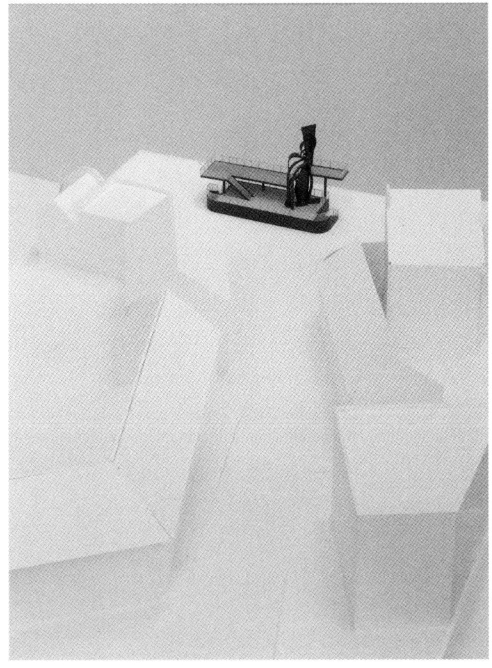

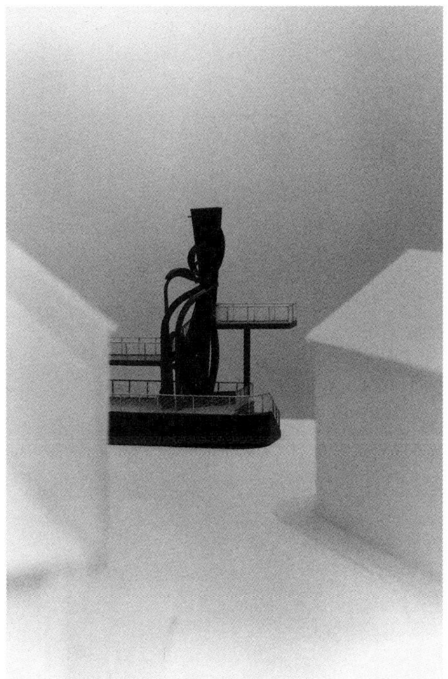

Small-scale model of *Sea Music* in situ on Poole Quay. Photo: John Riddy

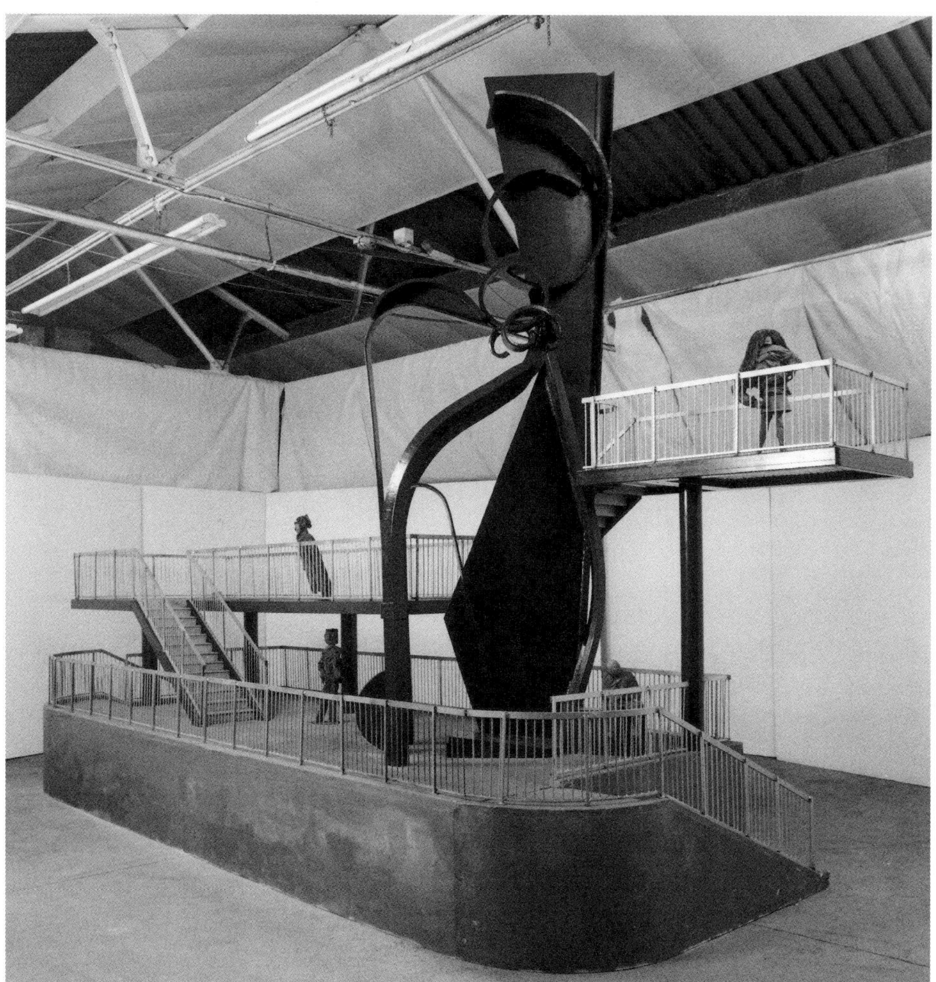

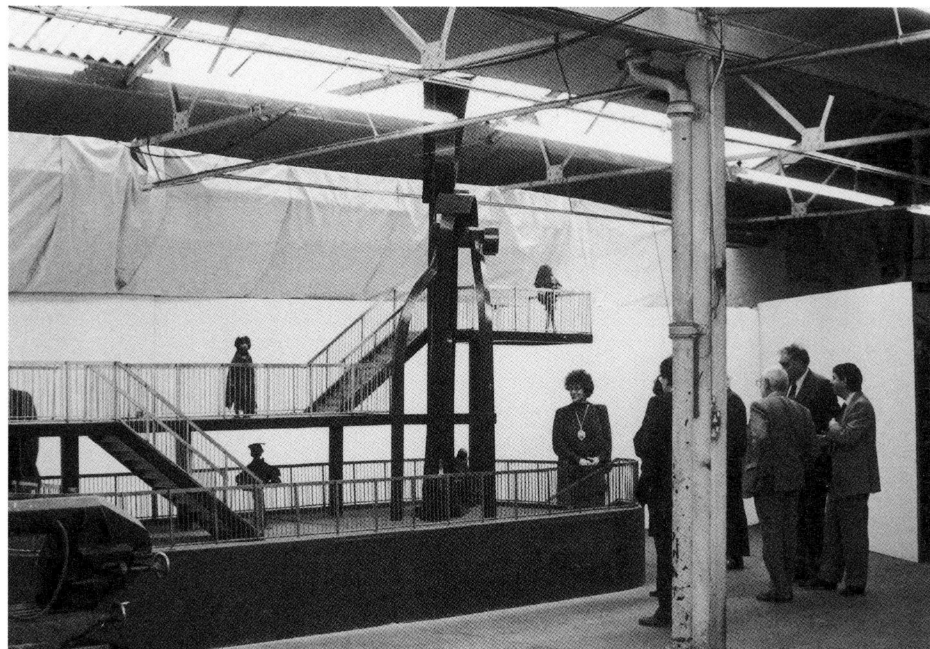

The final model for *Sea Music* in Caro's studio in 1991. Photo: John Riddy

Councillors from the Borough of Poole visiting Caro's studio in 1991.

Caro's endeavour and attention to detail while preparing for this meeting paid off. 'After a pleasant lunch', he recalled, 'we were happy that the Mayor and Councillors felt it would be a good thing to go ahead.' A letter from Ann Stribley, Poole's Mayor, dated 22 March 1991, confirmed the good news: 'We were delighted at the impressiveness of the work and its feel of "rightness" for the setting … We look forward with great interest to the unveiling of *Sea Music* in the autumn.' After months of intense activity working on the model for *Sea Music*, Caro could relax. From this moment, he reduced his direct involvement with the project. The one-third-size model was transported to Bourne Steel, where computer-generated drawings of it were produced, under the supervision of Poole's Assistant Borough Engineer Derrick Robinson, to aid its enlargement. The fabrication of *Sea Music* lasted around eighteen weeks, and passed with few hitches – any 'problems', Caro recalled, 'were clearly being met in an efficient and sensitive way'. Cunningham visited the steelworks on several occasions to advise on practical issues and to supervise progress. This allowed Caro to focus on other things, such as his exhibition at the Tate Gallery, which opened that October. The correspondence bears this out: there are no letters relating to *Sea Music* in the archives at Barford Sculptures between 22 March and 27 September. 'Our main involvement with the sculpture', Caro wrote later that year, 'recommenced as soon as it arrived on the Quay.' He was referring to the morning of 30 October, when, shortly after 7 am, *Sea Music* was manoeuvred into position, above the pumping station, by several cranes. Despite being so close to the finishing line, though, there were still more 'hurdles' to be negotiated. 'As I suspected', Caro wrote nine days after *Sea Music* had

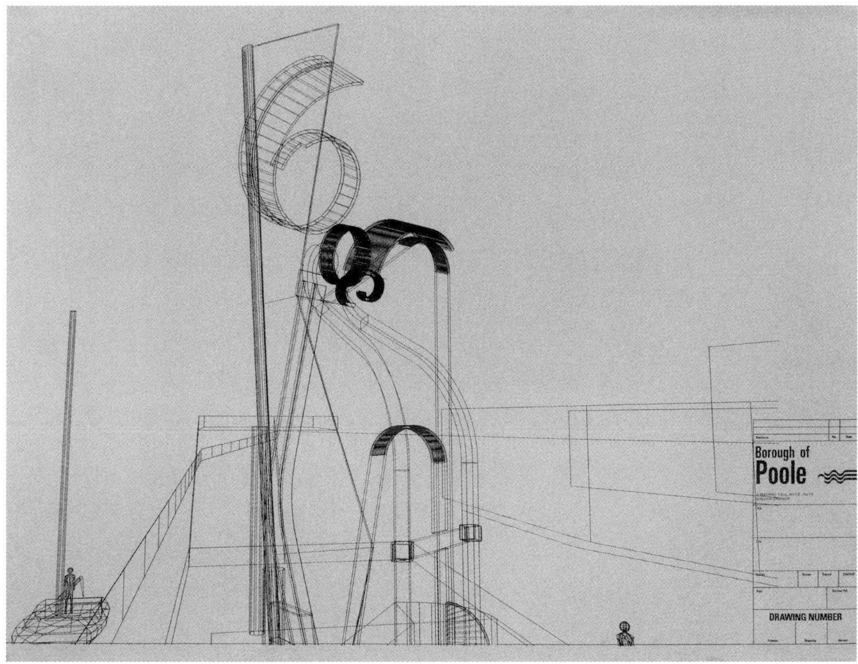

Elevation drawing of *Sea Music*.

been erected, 'certain changes were needed to make the sculpture look stronger against the sky. We made these alterations, but working on such big steel parts necessitated long delays. Cutting metal two inches thick, hoisting and welding each piece takes a long time and many hours and even days passed as each element was put together.' The welds on *Sea Music* had to be made 'stronger', so that it could 'withstand the force of the winds'. It was already galvanised, but the sculpture still required a last coat of paint, to 'provide the finishing colour and protection against rust and deterioration'. Caro ultimately chose a handsome blue (rather than the white that he had originally envisaged), having consulted his wife who regularly advised him on his use of colour. Readily evoking both the sea and the sky, this colour was entirely appropriate for the sculpture's setting.

Meanwhile, the walkways and staircases, which had been fabricated off-site, had not been installed. As late as 27 September, Caro and Roberts were still corresponding about the appearance of the seats and benches, as well as their materials: 'I feel it will be confusing', the artist wrote, 'if we design them too much.' The concrete pumping station was elegantly dressed with brick by a local building firm, Burt & Vick, who also provided decking and handrails for the walkways. Writing on 14 November, Roberts noted that, in total, 12 firms had contributed to the sculpture in terms of funding or labour. Thanks to their commitment, everything was finished in time for the official unveiling on 22 November. 'The result of all this enterprise', Roberts said, 'is the tallest sculpture, by far, which Sir Anthony Caro has ever produced and, in my opinion, one of his most exciting.' He continued, with satisfaction: 'It has been built entirely by local

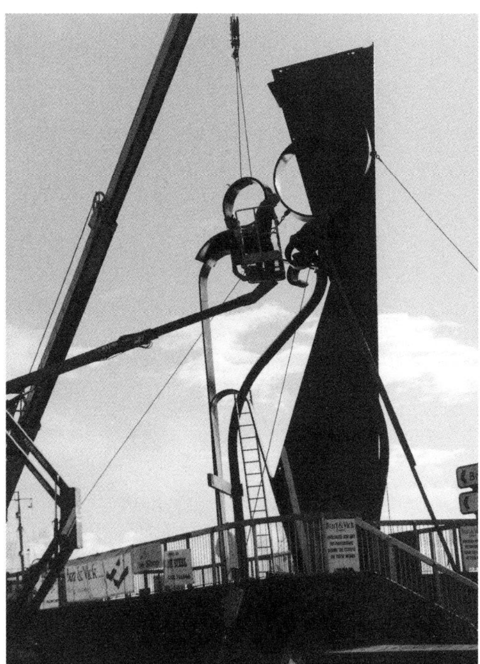

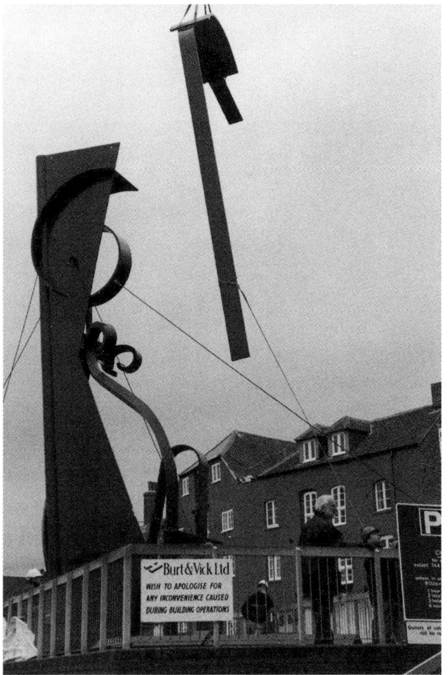

Installation of *Sea Music* in 1991.

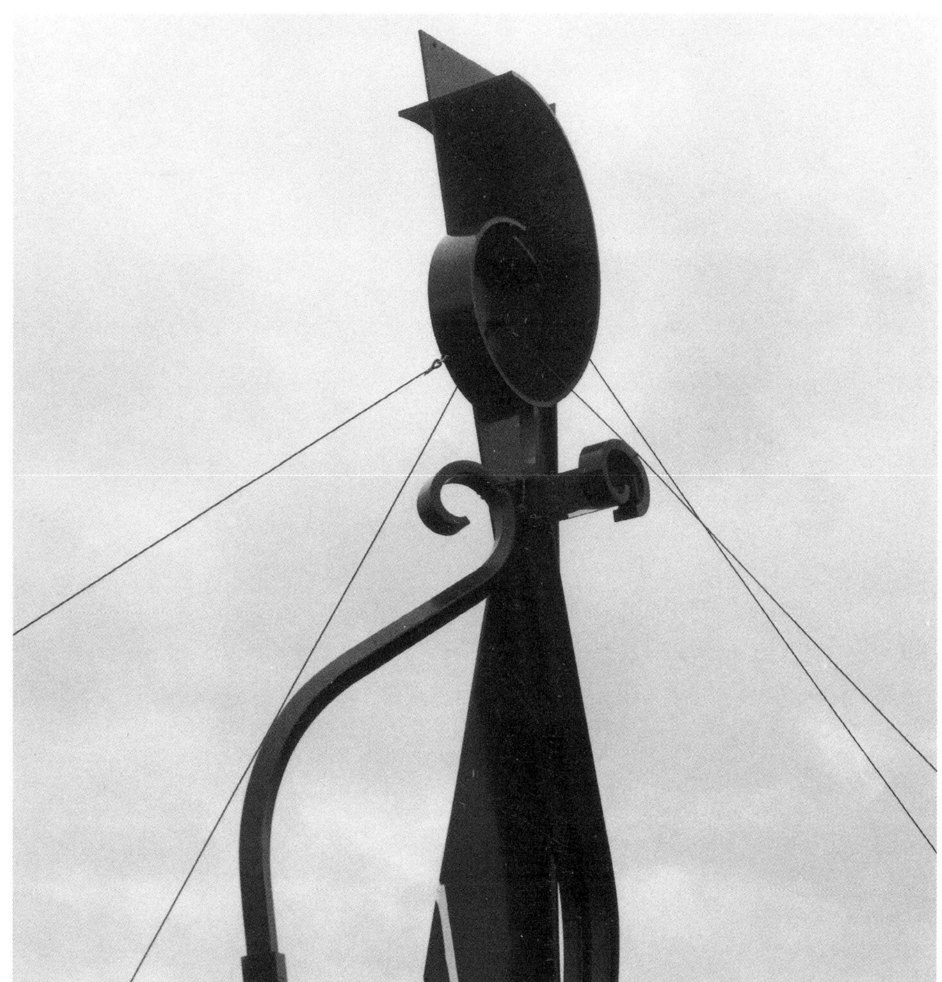

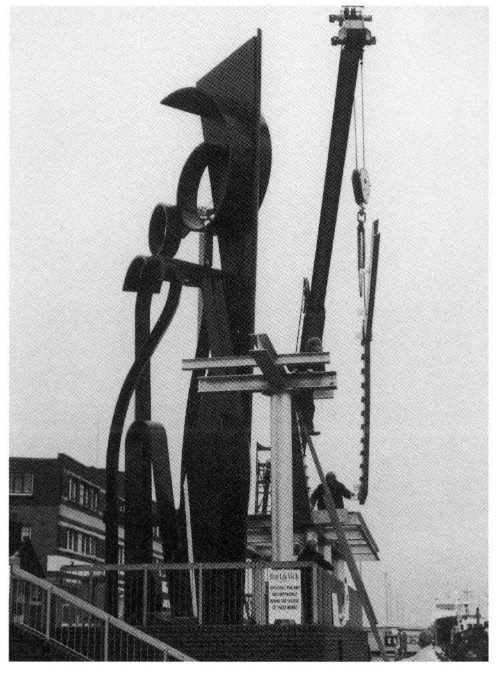

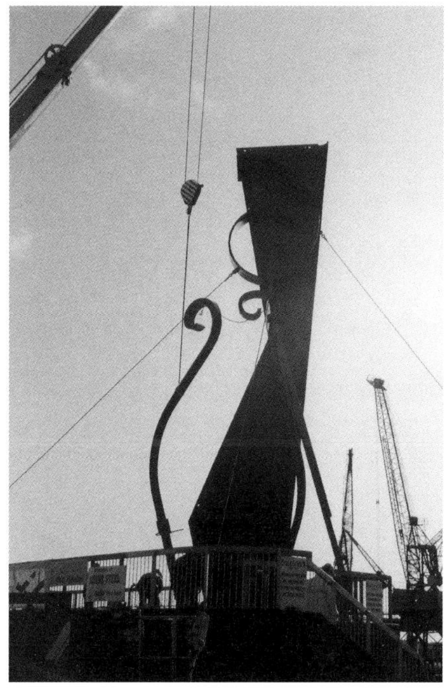

endeavour, by people proud of Poole, and as such the story of its achievement is as important as the work of art itself. It is a story which should be told, as an inspiration to all the other towns in Britain where such opportunities can and should be grasped.'

A quarter of a century on, the story of the 'achievement' of *Sea Music*, as inspirational as it is, has faded into history. The work of art, itself, though, will endure. In the archives at Barford Sculptures, there is a sheet of notes handwritten by Caro in preparation for a short speech that he gave at the launch of the sculpture in 1991. At the bottom, after a reminder to thank all those involved, the artist proposed a toast acknowledging Roberts's input: 'to the man whose initiative patience & determination have masterminded this entire operation'. It recorded the gratitude of a great artist who, while working on *Sea Music*, found himself at liberty to produce a piece of monumental public art in whatever manner he saw fit. Creating *Sea Music*, which was meant to 'raise the spirits', was as spontaneous and exciting, for Caro, as making public art could ever be.

Sea of Music: After Caro

Jim Aitchison

Responding to visual artworks in music has been central to my artistic work for nearly two decades. Subjects include Doris Salcedo's *Shibboleth* (2007) in the Turbine Hall at Tate Modern; new sculpture by Antony Gormley; Richard Deacon's work at Tate St Ives (2005) and the Henry Moore Institute (2007); and Anish Kapoor's exhibition at the Royal Academy of Arts (2009). *Sea Music* by Anthony Caro provided a new and compelling challenge.

Caro has been explicit in citing the significance of music to his sculpture. He needed to have music playing in his studio while he worked, and felt that there should be some kind of kinship – that the music shouldn't 'jar' with the unfolding artworks. When I went to visit Caro's Camden studio, I was amazed to discover the sculptor's vast music collection on CD and on vinyl, and it struck me that much of his sculpture was produced within a 'sea' of music. The renowned and uncompromising abstract artist had defined musical tastes, limited almost exclusively to the Baroque, Classical and Romantic eras. At the very least, one might have expected to find Stravinsky in his collection, but for the most part it was comprised of canonical European classics: Handel, Mozart, Beethoven, Schubert and Brahms. There was something surprising and deeply fascinating about art rooted in the twentieth century being connected in the mind of the artist with music from two or three hundred years before. That connection across disciplines and artistic ecologies was significant in the shaping of my response to *Sea Music*.

I wanted to engage with both the music that might have surrounded the sculpture's emergence in the studio, and the physical reality of *Sea Music* itself. Caro's appearance on the BBC's *Desert Island Discs* on Radio 4 in April 2000 provided a valuable insight into the music most important to him. I constructed an imaginary playlist from which I would harvest material, and then chose segments from three of Caro's favourite pieces: the first and last movements of Brahms's Fourth Symphony, the opening of Mozart's Piano Concerto no.20, and the slow movement from Caro's favourite piece of all, Schubert's String Quintet in C. My task was to then re-examine the sculpture, identify structures and qualities and attempt to pass the musical fragments I had selected through them as a kind of filter.

There is a complex interaction of simple shapes at play in *Sea Music*. Caro renders straight lines, curves and circles in steel, giving an impression of a dynamic fluid terrain. Viewers may well discern resonances with the visual apparatus of musical notation, but, simultaneously, these forms interact to evoke water in motion with a variety of wave shapes superimposed over each other and piled up into a tower. The viewing platforms provide a satisfying formal contrast, and enhance the sense of fluidity experienced by the viewer, as different perspectives are available at a variety of heights and angles.

I attempted to engage with these aspects in three sections. The first movement takes the presence and disposition of the platforms as a starting point, disposing three brass instruments of low to high pitch range as if physically present on the three levels, to perform the 'fanfare for Caro'. The music for this movement is derived from the eight chords of the chaconne from the opening of the finale of Brahms's Fourth Symphony, the highest pitches of which proceed upwards for the most part, in a stepwise motion.

The basis of the second movement is the interacting circles, curves and verticals, and the differing viewpoints. I selected a short segment of just four pitches from the opening of Brahms's Fourth Symphony, which 'grew' into longer strands, and which I could mould into musical forms reminiscent of Caro's creation of circles and verticals. A succession of pitches rendered into curved melodic lines occur throughout the movement, particularly in the woodwind. Similarly, the verticals, referencing the mast-like sections of *Sea Music*, can be simply conceived. However, things became more complex in other regards. I evoked a circle of sorts in the domain of harmony using the familiar device of transposing through a cycle; ending up back where one has begun suggests a kind of circular motion. The repetition of this cyclic pattern underpins much of the music, which has a structure that can be interpreted as an unyielding firm line. In the contrasting middle section, the cyclic material becomes subordinate to a plucked bass line – a texture somewhat reminiscent of Baroque models. The sense of a 'firm line' is absolutely foremost here, though I sought to undermine this at times through subtle rhythmic instability. In addition, the melodic 'curves' on solo clarinet and violin often trip over one another quite uncomfortably: a kind of slow motion evocation, for me, of Caro's tumbling curves and rings on the sculpture. The final section of this movement proposes an altered viewpoint of the sculpture by taking the material of the first section and repeating it backwards. I was taken by Caro's wish that *Sea Music* be 'an open free work, airy and fresh'. Accordingly, there is a lightness and sense of energy here, with layers and interlacing wave patterns. This is in contrast to the third and final movement.

In Schubert's String Quartet I found a new direction. I took a segment of melody from its slow movement and made a series of single line improvisations around it, always attempting to create short curves within the larger contours. A lengthy process of refining these rough 'takes' ensued, until I ended up with a contrapuntal texture presenting several different versions of these lines in simultaneous 'conversation'. The first section of the final movement is, in effect, a slow fugato, no longer playful but decidedly desolate in character. The middle section takes the same material but presents it starkly in multiple octaves across the strings, angular and disjointed, and accompanied by a restless web of overlapping, wave-like crescendi, the pitches of which are derived from the Brahms chaconne.

The final section has a brief reminiscence of the opening of the second movement, representing the tranquil culmination of the whole musical trajectory. Visiting Caro's studio felt both joyful and sad. The artist's presence was still tangible and the warmth and energy of the man radiated from the spaces of the studio; I wanted a sense of this to come through in the final movement. The initial dark, spare lines are built into a tapestry of multiple voices casting wave shapes at different speeds, transforming the bleak and restless chromatic colours of the opening to a glowing pitch continuum based on a simple overtone mode. Sounding above this texture is the trumpet, playing an altered version of the original segment of melody taken from Schubert's String Quintet.

Sea Music has soaked into my imagination. From its location overlooking Poole Quay, it exerts a force that transfers across boundaries.

The Concerto Series

Sculpture by Anthony Caro

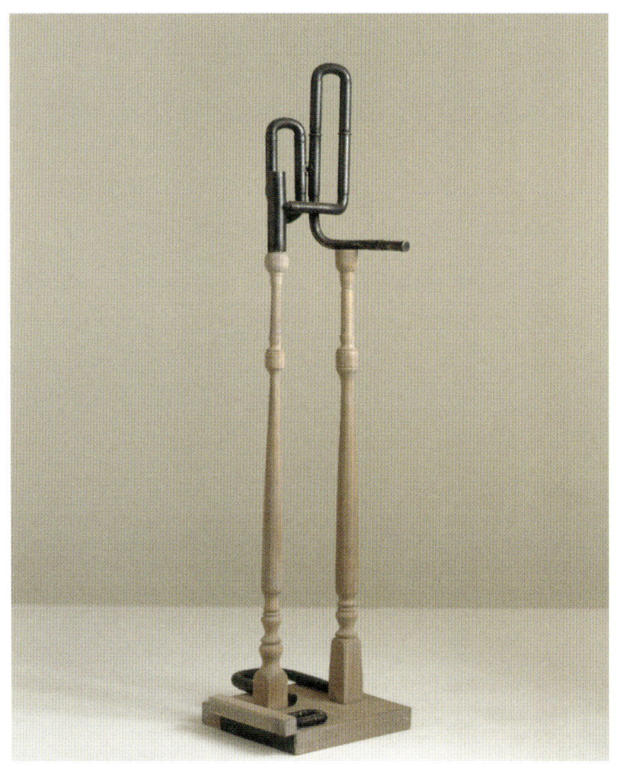

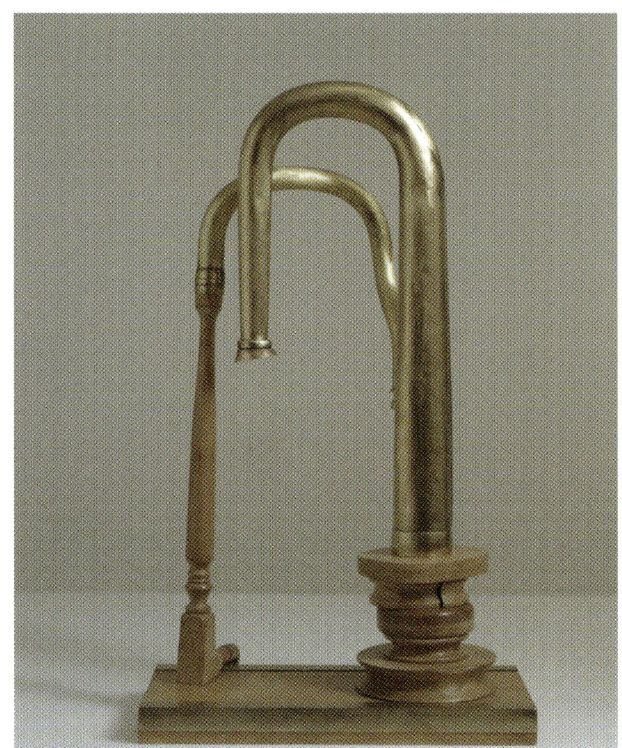

Alto Flute (Concerto series)
1999
Wood and brass
85 × 22 × 25.5 cm

Bassoon (Concerto series)
1999
Wood and brass
72 × 42 × 23 cm

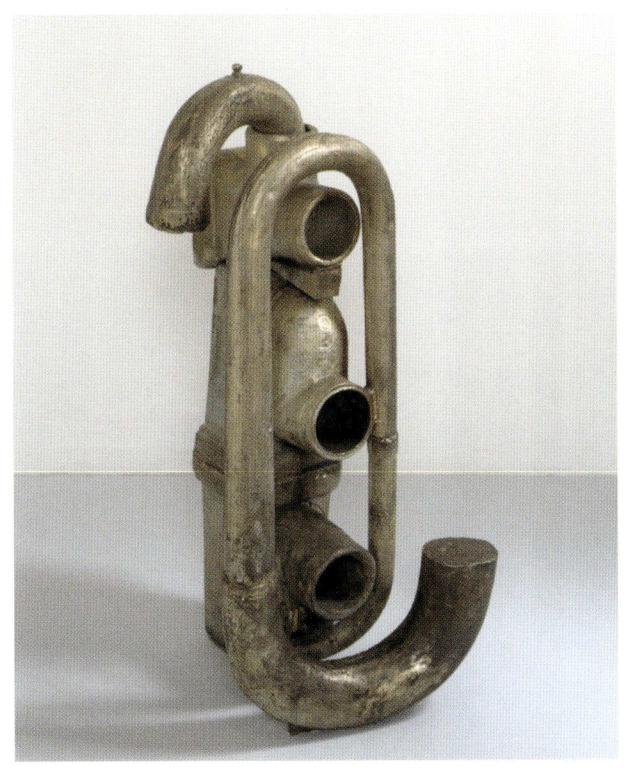

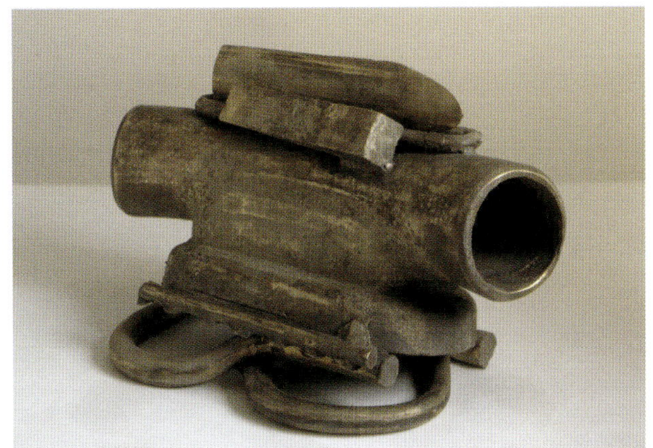

Baritone (Concerto series)
2000
Cast and welded brass
99 × 47 × 49.5 cm

Bolero (Concerto series)
1999
Cast brass
32 × 53.5 × 28 cm

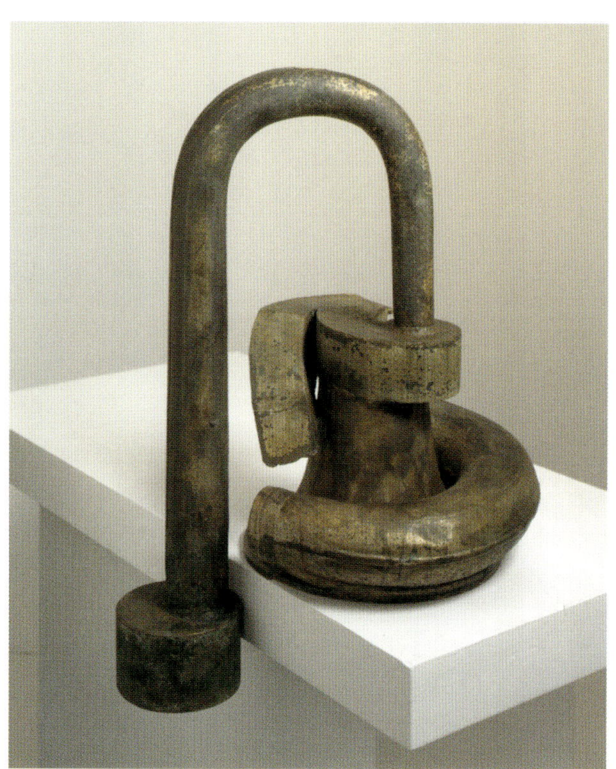

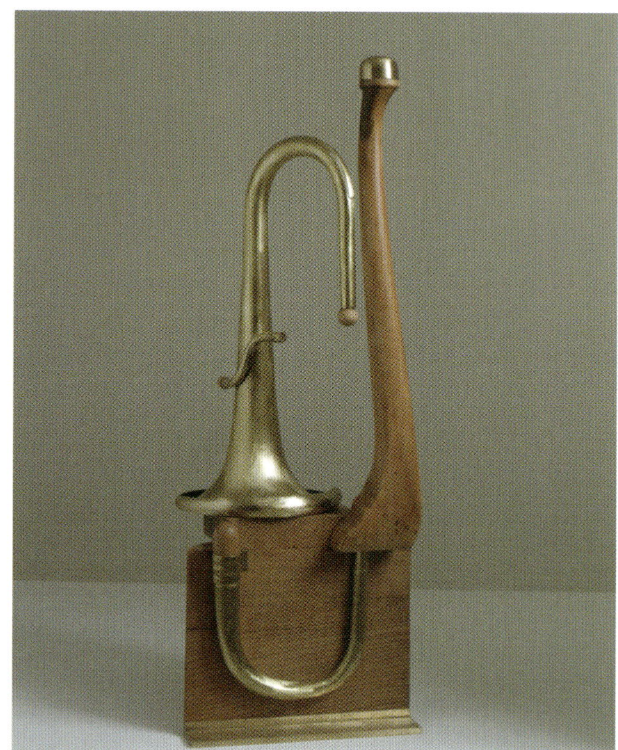

Crescendo (Concerto series)
2000
Cast and welded brass and bronze
73.5 × 37 × 53 cm

Double Bass (Concerto series)
1999
Wood and brass
86.5 × 30.5 × 23 cm

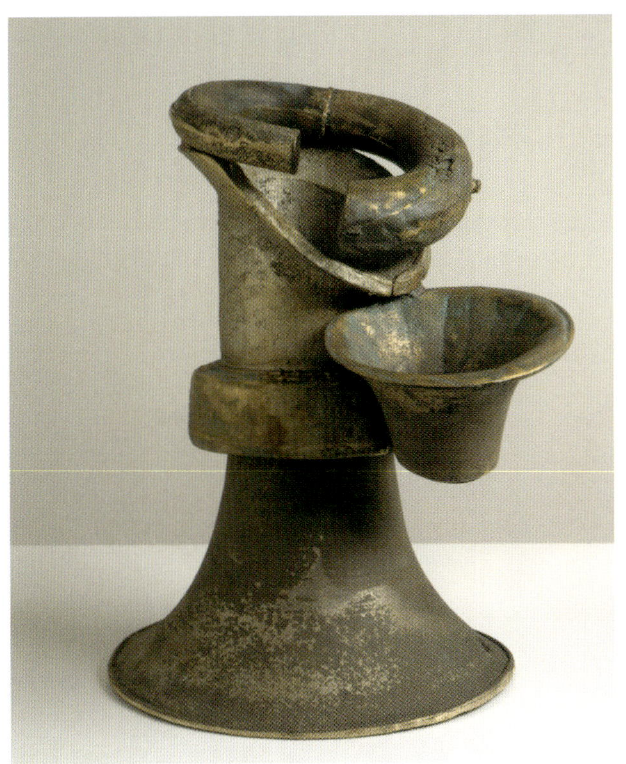

Euphonium (Concerto series)
2000
Cast brass
62 × 43.5 × 54 cm

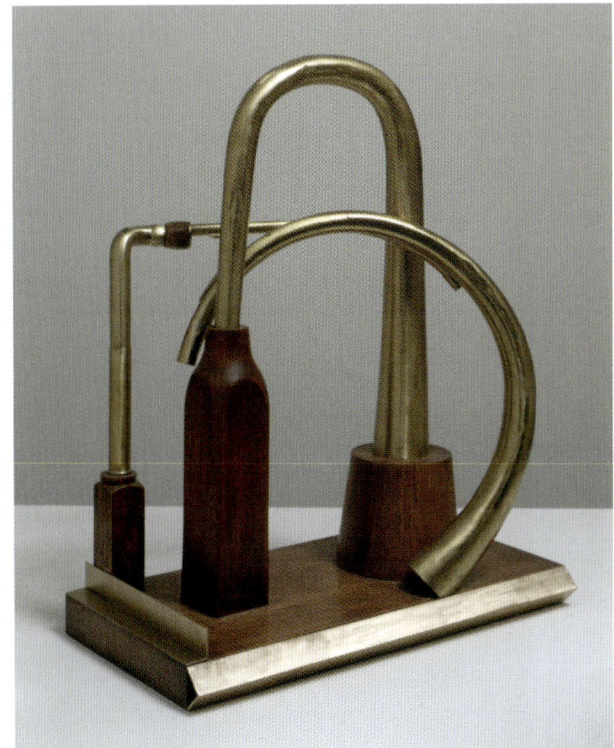

French Horn (Concerto series)
2000
Brass and wood
52 × 43.5 × 25 cm

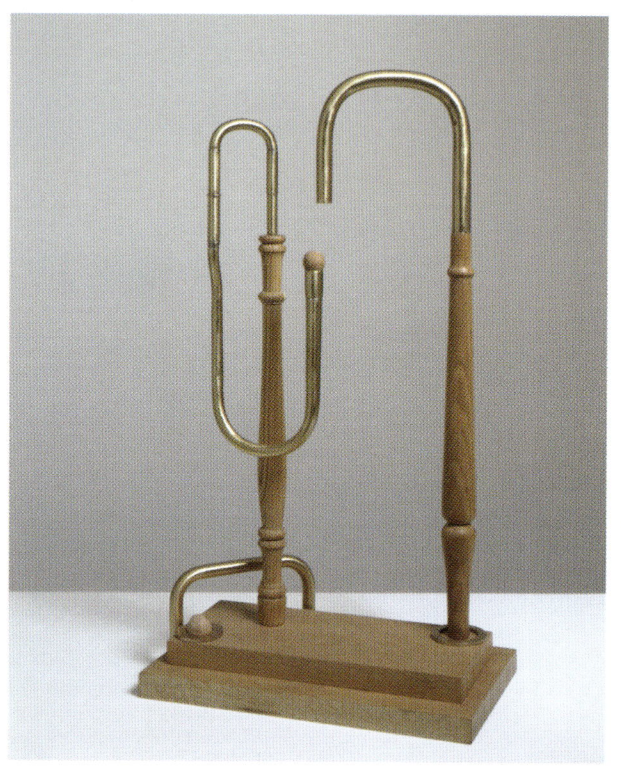

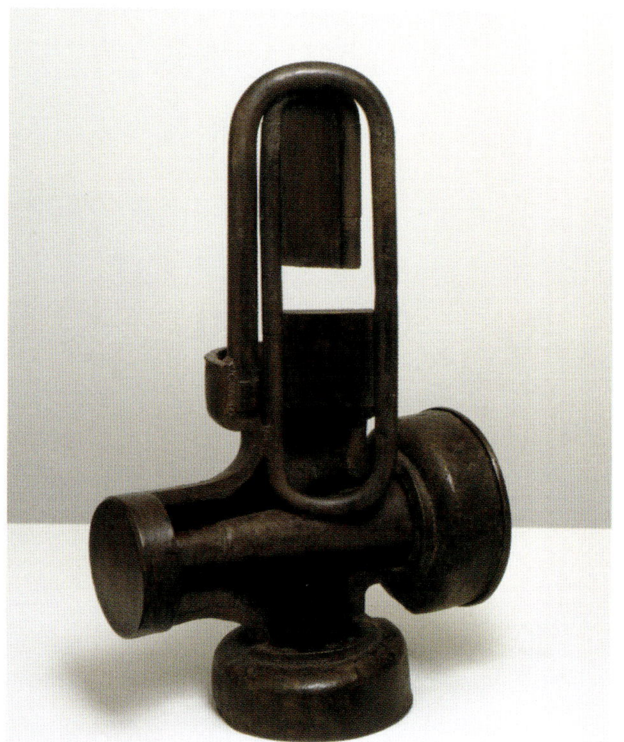

Horn Duet (Concerto series)
2000
Brass and wood
69 × 38 × 21 cm

Mezzo Forte (Concerto series)
1999–2000
Brass
62 × 37 × 23 cm

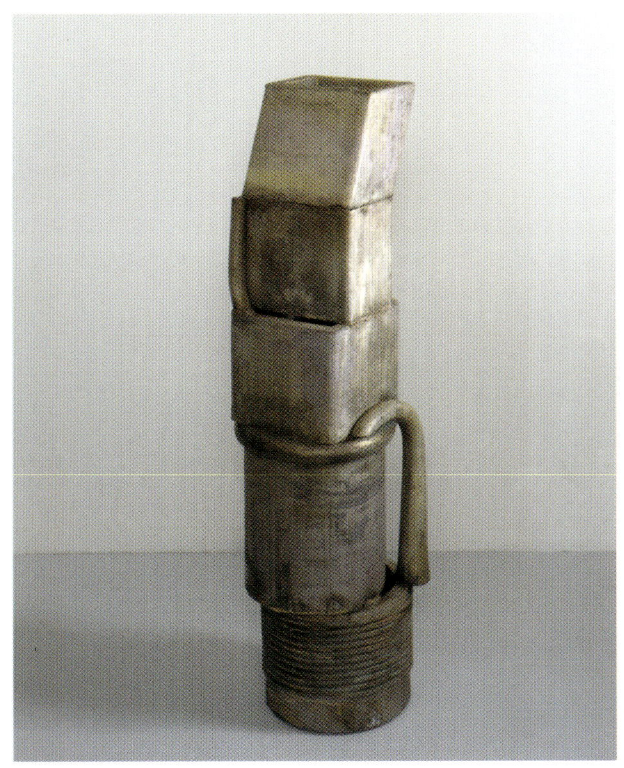

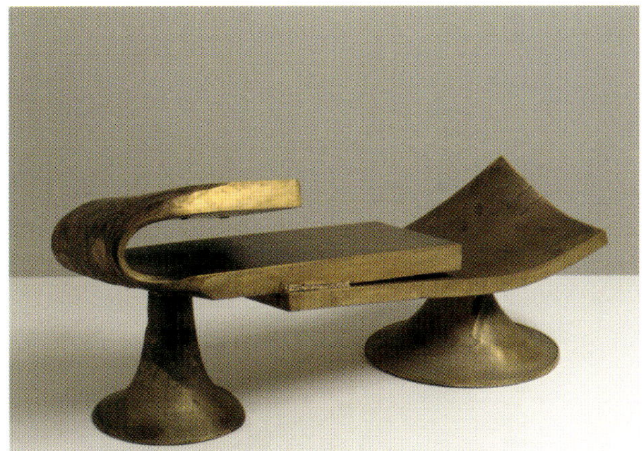

Percussion (Concerto series)
2000
Cut and welded brass
110.5 × 28 × 25.5 cm

Plainsong (Concerto series)
2000
Cut and welded brass
35 × 85 × 32 cm

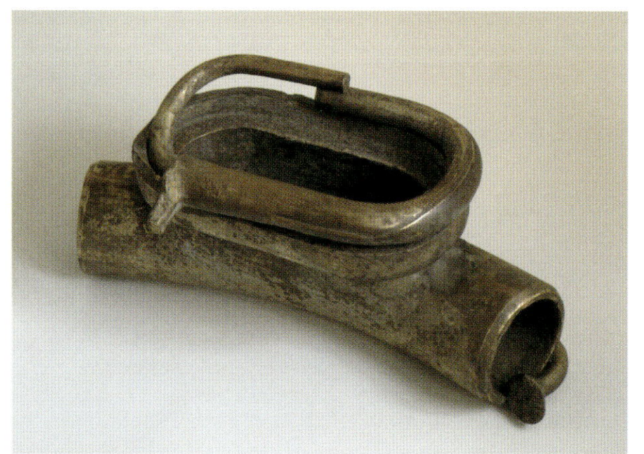

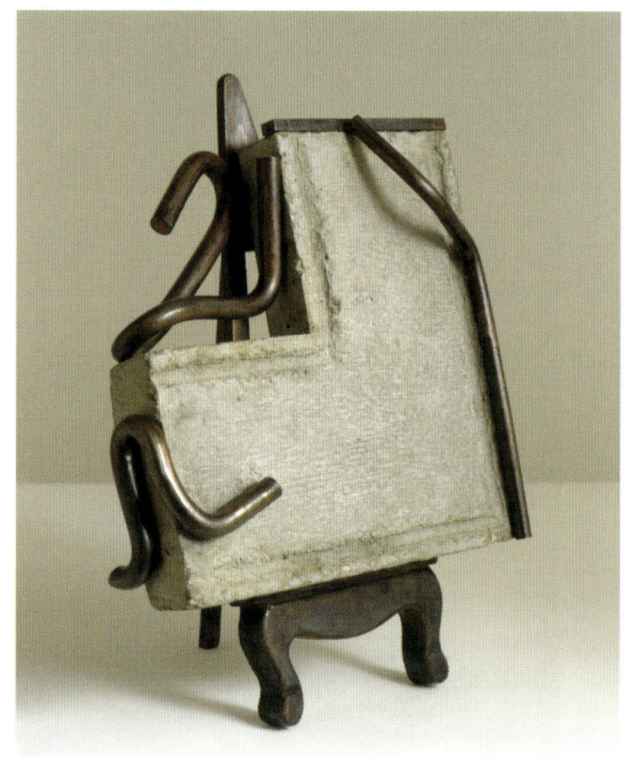

Ritenuto (Concerto series)
1999
Cast brass
23 × 53.5 × 27 cm

Sonatina (Concerto series)
1999
Cement and cast, welded and patinated brass
34 × 32 × 22 cm

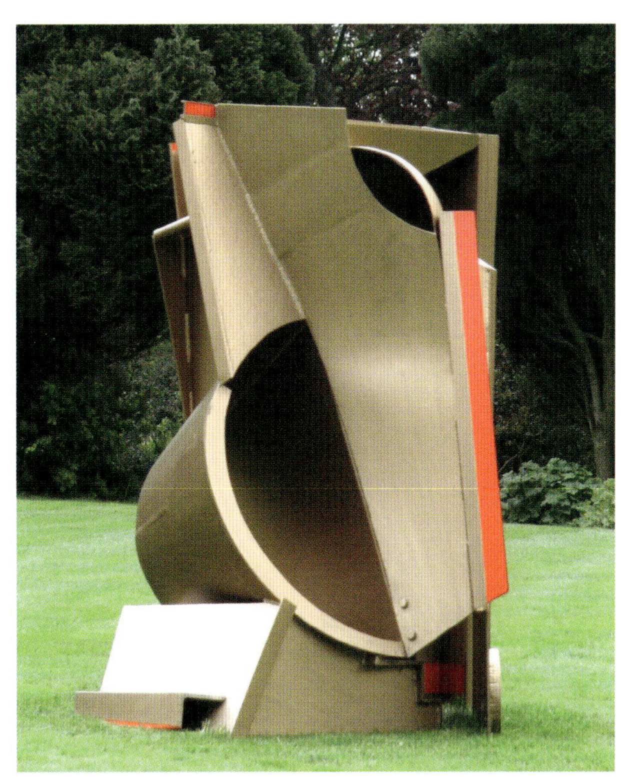

Slow March
1985
Painted steel
208.5 × 145 × 155 cm

Published by Ridinghouse in 2017 to coincide with the conservation of Anthony Caro's *Sea Music* on Poole Quay and the exhibitions in Poole Museum of Caro's Concerto series and David Ward's *One Hundred Views of Sea Music* from 13 May – 15 October 2017 curated by Stephen Feeke, Director of the New Art Centre, Roche Court.

Ridinghouse
46 Lexington Street
UK – London W1F 0LP
ridinghouse.co.uk

In association with
New Art Centre
Roche Court
East Winterslow
Salisbury
UK – Wiltshire SP5 1BG
sculpture.uk.com

Distributed in the UK and Europe by
Cornerhouse Publications
c/o Home
2 Tony Wilson Place
UK – Manchester M15 4FN
cornerhousepublications.org

Distributed in the US by
RAM Publications + Distribution, Inc.
2525 Michigan Avenue Building A2
US – Santa Monica, CA 90404
rampub.com

Edited by Stephen Feeke
Proofread by Dorothy Feaver
Designed by Marit Münzberg
Printed in the UK by Henry Ling Limited

ISBN 978 1 909932 37 1

This publication would not have been possible without the generous support of The Heritage Lottery Fund, Barford Sculptures Ltd and the New Art Centre, Roche Court Sculpture Park.

For the awards to repair, conserve and celebrate *Sea Music*, we are indebted to the Heritage Lottery Fund and to Arts Council England for additional support using public funding through the National Lottery.

A collaborative venture such as this, involves many people to bring it to fruition and additional thanks go to: Judy Adam; Jim Aitchison; Denise Andrews; Olivia Bax; Madeleine Bertorelli; Beth Biddiss; Stephen Bishop; Debra Bodman; Stacy Boldrick; Sarah Boling of Sarah Boling Associates; Erica Bolton; John Bowen; Maurice Braganza; Julius Bryant; Rosalind Conlon; Paul Caro; Sarah Cope of The Cast; Charlotte Colombo; Suzanne Deal Booth; Catherine Croft; Gautier Deblonde; The Worshipful Mayor of Poole, Councillor Xena Dion; Bill Dow; Ellie Douglas; Jane Foley of Jane Foley Associates; Doro Globus; Charlotte Glyde; Antony Gormley; George Gower; Dr Brian Graham; the team at Hall Conservation Ltd; Kelly Spry-Phare; Ellen Dempster, Victoria Allott of Heritage Lottery Fund South West; Chris Holloway; Sian Hutchings; Felicity Irwin; Councillor Mohan Iyengar; Laura Joy; John Kerley; Janet Mein; Olga Midgley; Hattie Miles; Sonia Mills; David and Audrey Mirvish; Mary Moore; Peter Murray; Molly Nickson; Michele O'Brien; Jonathan Parsons; Claire Wade and the team at Poole Housing Partnership; Anne Simpson at Poole Tourism; Tom Rowland; Christine Rowley; Rebecca Sampson; Katie Sayles; Ali Sharpe; Denise Poote; Dasha Shenkman; Anne Sieve; Alastair Sooke; Andrew & Tricia Creamer at The Spire; The Deputy Mayor of Poole Councillor Ann Stribley; Sile Stuttard; Jenny Surridge; Lizzie Sykes; Lisa Tregale of Bournemouth Symphony Orchestra; Nigel Walters at Troika; Lewis Walker; Wessex Water; David Ward; Richard Waring; Paul White; Nicky Whittenham; Kim Wide of Take a Part; Clare Winterbottom; and Godfrey Worsdale.

We are grateful to Lord Palumbo for agreeing to formally relaunch *Sea Music* in 2017, having originally launched it in 1991. Thanks are also due to the members of the Sea Music Project Board: Michael Armstrong; Patrick Cunningham; Emma Kerr; Michael Spender; Stephen Feeke; Tom Roberts; and especially to the Project Manager Melinda McCheyne.

Cover: *Sea Music* by Anthony Caro from David Ward's series of photographs *One Hundred Views of Sea Music* (2016–17).

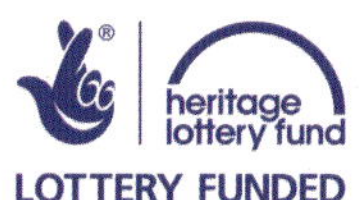

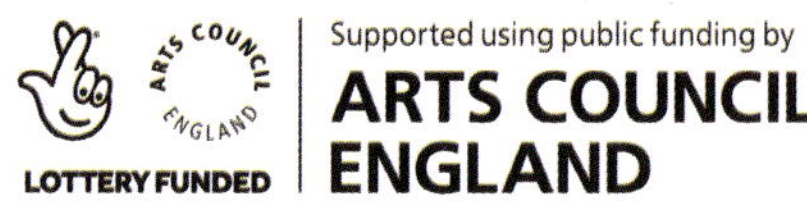

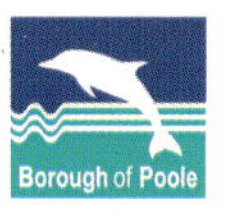

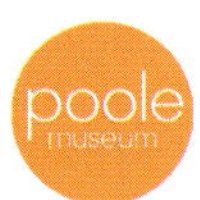

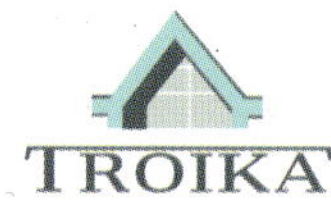

Ridinghouse
NewArtCentre.